LEARN TO PLAY DRUMS
THE COMPLETE DRUM METHOD VOLUME 2

Discover Bass Drum Patterns, Two-hand Accents, Displacements, Triplets & Ride Lines

DARYL INGLETON

FUNDAMENTAL CHANGES

Learn to Play Drums: The Complete Drum Method Volume 2

Discover Bass Drum Patterns, Two-hand Accents, Displacements, Triplets & Ride Lines

Published by **www.fundamental-changes.com**

ISBN 978-1-78933-027-4

www.fundamental-changes.com

Twitter: **@guitar_joseph**

Over 10,000 fans on Facebook: **FundamentalChangesInGuitar**

Instagram: **FundamentalChanges**

For over 350 Free Guitar Lessons with Videos Check Out

www.fundamental-changes.com

Cover Image Copyright: Uximetc pavel

Contents

Introduction

Welcome to *Learn to Play Drums Volume 2: Essential Drum Kit Studies*. This is the second in a two-book series that has been created to guide new drummers through fundamental drum techniques and playing concepts.

Each book contains ten lessons which will provide you with all the knowledge and skills needed to grow your understanding of drumming and playing ability.

My aim is that, upon completing these books, you will be armed with enough skill and technique to get serious about a career in music.

I came up with the concept for these books while I was working professionally on the London music scene. At the time, I was talking to and performing with many other drummers of varied experience and training. Some had a high level of training, others had limited training, and some were completely self-taught. All of them had lots of passion for what they were doing, but I noticed that only the drummers with a high level of training had the technique and drumming vocabulary to truly express themselves.

When I talked to drummers who were self-taught, they would generally enquire about the techniques and concepts I was using – which I gladly shared. I would usually encourage them to take lessons or pursue studying through a music school, but there were often financial barriers to this. As an alternative, I would recommend books or online tuition videos. The usual response to this was that they felt overwhelmed by the sheer volume of online tuition that was available and didn't know where to begin.

This is when I decided to create these books, to give drummers a comprehensive knowledge of the essential techniques and concepts in a guided environment. By the time you've completed these lessons, my hope is that you'll have the drumming vocabulary to express yourself on your instrument, regardless of the style of music you love to play. The path to becoming a great drummer is long, but it is incredibly worthwhile.

How to Use This Book

This book is divided into ten lessons. Each begins with a lesson plan explaining the lesson's objectives and how they will be achieved. They are organised to give you information about theory and playing through exercises and repetition.

If you are a beginner...

Work through each lesson one at a time. Start by reading the lesson plan. Understand what the objectives are and how they will be achieved. Then work through the lesson. When you have finished a lesson, make sure you rehearse and practise all you've learned before moving on to the next one.

If you are already a drummer...

Read through the book from beginning to end, focusing on the parts that cover material that is new to you. Read the text and practise the exercises in these parts. Ensure that you rehearse the material well before you continue to the next lesson.

If you are a tutor teaching from this book...

Read the entire book. Ensure that you are familiar with every aspect of the content before you begin teaching it yourself. You can use this book as a curriculum, but you will have to gauge the level of your student and adapt it accordingly.

Right- or Left-handed...

This book series is written for the right-handed player. If you are left-handed you have two choices:

It is possible to use this teaching just as it is presented and learn the drums as a right-handed player. Alternatively, you will need to invert the information. In other words, every time a RIGHT is indicated, you will play a LEFT – and vice versa.

Remember that you will get out of this book what you put into it. Work steadily through the lessons, complete the tasks, and keep an eye on the tips and suggestions. Keep in mind that one of the key tools in learning an instrument is repetition.

Suggestions for Independent Study

Schedule Your Practice

Scheduling practice time is very beneficial for learning an instrument. I recommend that you allocate yourself set time slots during the week for your practice sessions. You don't have to follow a rigid regime if you don't want to, but make sure you allow yourself time to rehearse, practise and continue your development.

Playing Proficiency

- Don't be tempted to skip the text in each lesson – it contains valuable information needed to understand that lesson. If you skim over it, you will be missing out on necessary knowledge

- If you are struggling to play something, break it down into smaller parts. Learning the vocabulary of drums is similar to learning to pronounce a new word. Break it down into its syllables. Do this with all the drum parts you find difficult

- Play slowly. It is important to play slowly when encountering new ideas. Playing at a slower tempo allows you to truly understand the task at hand. When you are comfortable at a slower tempo, only then increase to a faster one. You cannot play something fast if you cannot play something slow!

- Play in front of a mirror. This will help you to analyse your body movements and position. It will help to ensure that your posture is correct and your movements are symmetrical

- Record yourself. If you own any type of recording device, such as a video camera, tape recorder, mobile phone etc., then record yourself playing. Play it back and listen to it. This is a great way to analyse your playing and keep a record of your progression

Reading and Writing Notation Proficiency

- Pay attention to all the information regarding notes in this book

- Practise writing notes by copying the exercises in this book

Repetition

You will achieve a higher level of proficiency in drumming if you repeat the exercises and drum phrasing as often as possible. It doesn't always have to be on a drum kit – you can use a practice pad or even tap on your legs

Listening

It is important to listen to music as often as possible. As your drumming knowledge grows you will be able to analyse what the drummer is doing on a record. This will give you new ideas and open the door to more playing possibilities.

What You Will Need:

Standard Four-Piece Drum Kit

This includes:

Snare drum

Bass drum

Top tom

Floor tom

Hi-Hat

Ride

Crash

Drum stool

Hardware for these elements

Sticks

There are many sticks on the market; find a pair that you find comfortable to hold.

Practice Pad

These are usually round and made of rubber. The practice pad is designed for quieter practice.

Music Stand

This is for holding your music, so you can play and read easily.

Digital Metronome

Use this to practise your time-keeping.

Lesson One – 1/16th Note Bass Drum Grooves, Heel Up Foot Technique, Dotted Notation

Lesson Overview

The main objective of this lesson is to introduce 1/16th note bass drum patterns while playing grooves on the rest of the kit. We will explore the notation skills and specific techniques needed to master this subject. 1/16th note bass drum patterns rely heavily on *dotted notation*, so this is where we will begin.

Once these concepts are understood we will look at how to utilize them in our playing through progressive exercises and musical examples that build both your technique and musicality.

1/16th note bass drum grooves can be difficult to play at first. But they are great fun once you get the hang of them. They give you access to many rhythmic possibilities and allow you to create exciting grooves and rhythms.

Let's get started!

Dotted Notation

Dotted notes are widely used in drum music to create new note durations. Once you've learned how they work, you'll find that they simplify written music and make it clearer to read.

Adding a dot to a note signifies that its note duration has increased by 50%.

This is a dotted 1/4 note. A dotted 1/4 note has the duration of 1 and a 1/2 beats. This is because a 1/4 note has the duration of 1 beat and the dot increases its length by 50%.

Note —— ♩. —— Dot

Below is a chart that shows standard notes and their durations along with their dotted equivalents.

Note Name	Note	Duration	Dotted Note	Dotted Duration
whole note	𝅝	4 beats	𝅝.	6 beats
1/2 note	𝅗𝅥	2 beats	𝅗𝅥.	3 beats
1/4 note	♩	1 beat	♩.	1 1/2 beats
1/8th note	♪	1/2 beat	♪.	3/4 beat
1/16th note	𝅘𝅥𝅯	1/4 beat	𝅘𝅥𝅯.	3/8 beats

Dotted Rests

Dotted rests work in the same way as dotted notes. The dot is written after the rest and increases its duration by 50%

Rest Name	Rest	Duration	Dotted Note	Dotted Duration
whole note	𝄻	4 beats	𝄻.	6 beats
1/2 note	𝄼	2 beats	𝄼.	3 beats
1/4 note	𝄽	1 beat	𝄽.	1 1/2 beats
1/8th note	𝄾	1/2 beat	𝄾.	3/4 beat
1/16th note	𝄿	1/4 beat	𝄿.	3/8 beats

Dotted Noted Reading

Now you understand the concept of dotted notes, it's time to start reading and practising them.

Each of the following exercises is two bars long. The first bar is notated without dots, and the second bar shows the same rhythm notated using dots. This will teach you how dots simplify what's written, without affecting the sound of the rhythm.

Tips

- Read the exercises before playing

- Work out where the dots are and what they mean before playing

- If you are unsure of the length of any dotted note, use the chart on the previous page

- Remember that the dot increases a notes length by 50%

Example 1a:

Heel Up Foot Technique

There are a various foot techniques used when playing the drums, each of which has a different effect on volume and speed. In my previous book, the heel down technique was studied. This is a great technique to start with as it allows more stability for beginners. However, it's not suitable for all aspects of playing. This section will study another foot technique: the *heel up* technique.

Heel Up Technique

The heel up method allows for greater volume and faster, more powerful playing. This technique is more widely used in modern playing than the heel down method because it has wider applications and gives the bass drum a sharper, stronger sound.

Constructing the Resting Position for Heel Up Technique

- Place the heel of the foot on the butt plate of the foot pedal. The foot is in line with the pedal, and the beater is against the bass drum skin.

- Raise the heel about 3cm off the butt plate, while keeping the toes on the pedal and the bass drum beater against the bass drum skin. This should put the foot roughly parallel with the floor.

- This is called the *resting position* and is the starting position for the heel up method. It is where the foot should be when it is not playing.

Movement Analysis of Heel Up Technique and Foot Motion

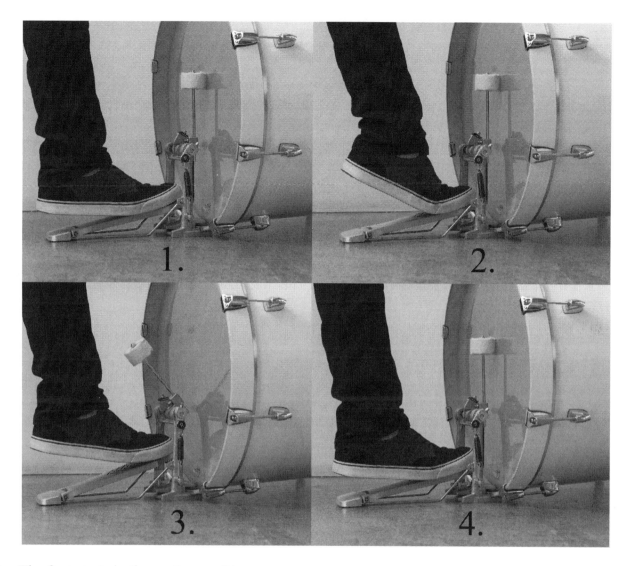

1. The foot starts in the resting position.

2. Raise the heel about 2-3cm, keeping the toes on the pedal and the bass drum beater against the bass drum skin.

3. Raise the toes about 2-3cm, keeping the heel where it is and the toes on the pedal. This action will allow the beater to pull away from the bass drum skin.

4. Drop the foot back in the resting position. This action will cause the beater to strike the bass drum skin.

The motion of the heel up technique is a bit like hopping. It is controlled mostly by the ankle and the calf muscle, so be aware not to raise your leg with your thigh muscle, as this can hinder the fluidity of the movements. It is common for your toes to lift off the pedal. This is not especially negative, but should avoided as any separation between you and the pedal minimises your efficiency and control.

When practising this technique, notice that all the movements work together to create a fluid motion that produces an excellent sound with great control.

Playing Heel Up Technique

Now you have learnt the basics of the heel up technique it is time to put it into action.

The first four exercises are on the bass drum and the second four exercises are on the hi-hat. Play each exercise on until you are comfortable with the motion of heel up technique.

Tips

- Play each exercise slowly
- Make sure you are following the correct heel up method
- Make sure the motions are fluid

Example 1b:

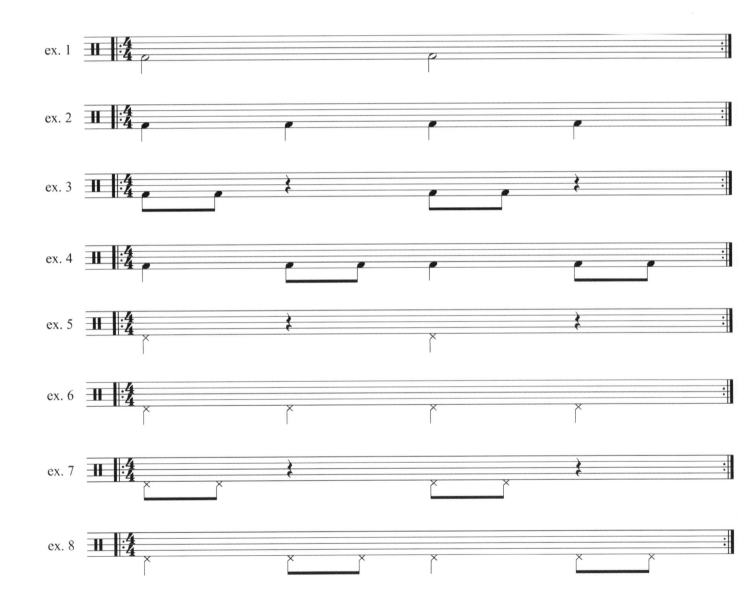

1/16th Note Bass Drum Grooves in 2/4

Now you understand both the heel up technique and dotted notes, it's time to start exploring this lesson's main objective: 1/16th note bass drum grooves. These grooves are common in drumming and it's important that you understand how to construct and play them.

To master 1/16th note based bass drum grooves we will learn the twenty-three different 1/16th note bass drum rhythms that fit inside two beats. These twenty-three rhythms are commonly referred to as the *fatback* exercises and are often used to study many other drumming concepts. With these twenty-three bars of 2/4 you can create 529 different bass drum combinations in a bar of 4/4. They're an important tool to help you master the drums.

These exercises consist of constant 1/8th note hi-hats, backbeat on the snare, and 1/16th note bass drum rhythms. Exercises one to sixteen show all the possible bass drum rhythms you can play before the snare. Exercises seventeen to twenty-three are all the possible bass drum rhythms you can play after the snare.

Tips

- Play each exercise slowly until you are comfortable with it

- Exercises with three or more continuous bass drums (i.e. ex. 15) are strenuous to play. Play these slowly at first

- Focus on using the heel up method

Bass Drum Rhythms Before the Backbeat

Example 1c:

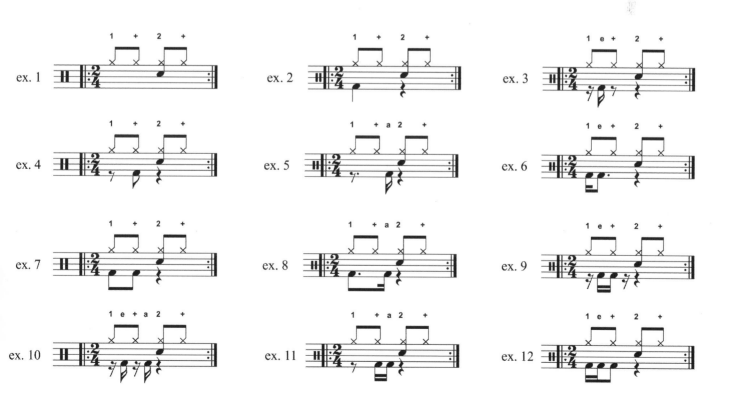

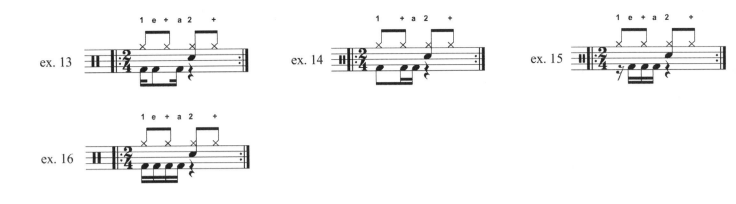

Bass Drum Rhythms After the Backbeat

Example 1d:

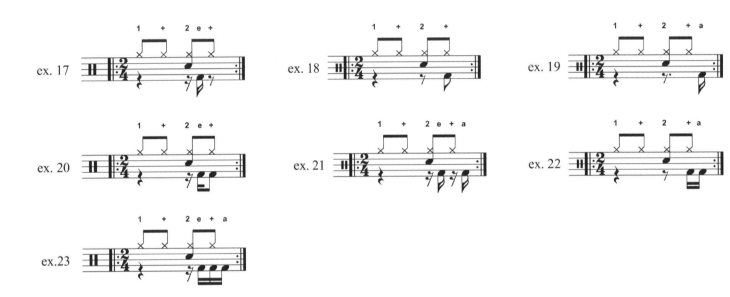

1/16th Note Bass Drum Grooves in 4/4

Below are twenty-two exercises in 4/4. Each 4/4 bar on this page is a combination of two of the 2/4 bars from the previous pages. Play each exercise until you are comfortable with it. Use a metronome to gradually increase your speed and confidence before you move on. Listen to the audio tracks to make sure you're playing these ideas correctly.

Tips

- Play each exercise slowly until you are comfortable with it

- Make sure you are using the heel up method

- Read the exercises and work out where the bass drum is placed before playing

Example 1e:

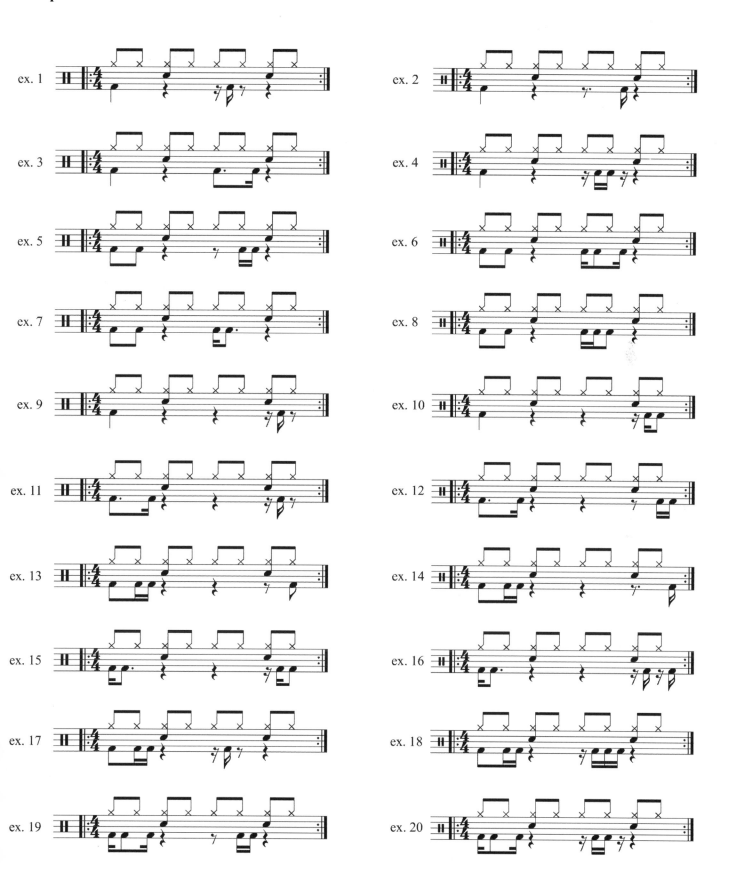

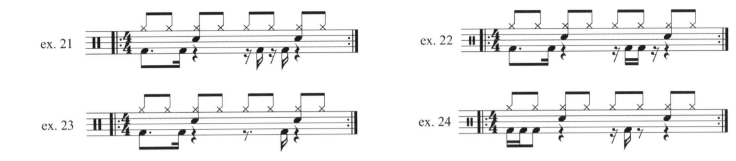

ex. 21   ex. 22

ex. 23   ex. 24

Constructing 1/16th Note Bass Drum Grooves in 4/4

Learning to construct your own grooves is an important skill to develop. It will help build your creativity and allow you to discover the grooves you want to play.

Task: Create at least ten different grooves in 4/4 by combining the 2/4 exercises from the previous 2/4 section.

Tips

Read through all the exercises from 1/16th Note Bass Drum Grooves in 2/4 and find the ones you want to combine.

Write them down so you can see them completed. Play through them and see how they sound; there are no wrong answers.

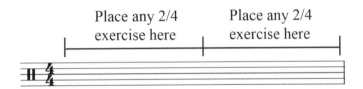

Place any 2/4 exercise here   Place any 2/4 exercise here

Merging 1/16th Note Bass Drum Grooves in 2/4

Here we will explore the concept of merging the 1/16th Note Bass Drum Grooves in 2/4. In that section there were two groups of exercises:

- Bass Drum Rhythms Before the Backbeat

- Bass Drum Rhythms After the Backbeat

So far we have played them as separate exercises, before combining them to create grooves in 4/4. Now we will merge the bass drum rhythms *before* and *after* the backbeat.

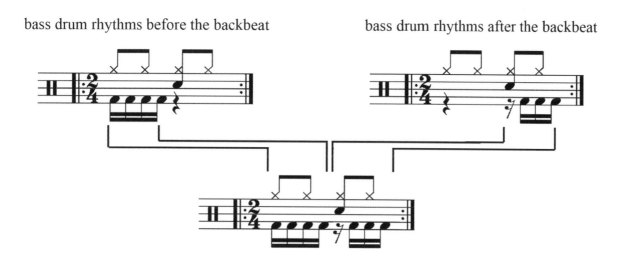

This approach allows you to create more rhythmic and groove possibilities.

Below are 24 exercises in 2/4. Each bar on this page is an example of a combination of the 1/16th Note Bass Drum Grooves in 2/4.

Play each exercise until you are comfortable with it and use a metronome to gradually speed up the examples.

Tips

- Play each exercise slowly until you are comfortable with it

- Make sure you are using the heel up method

- Read the exercises and work out where the bass drum is placed before playing

Example 1f:

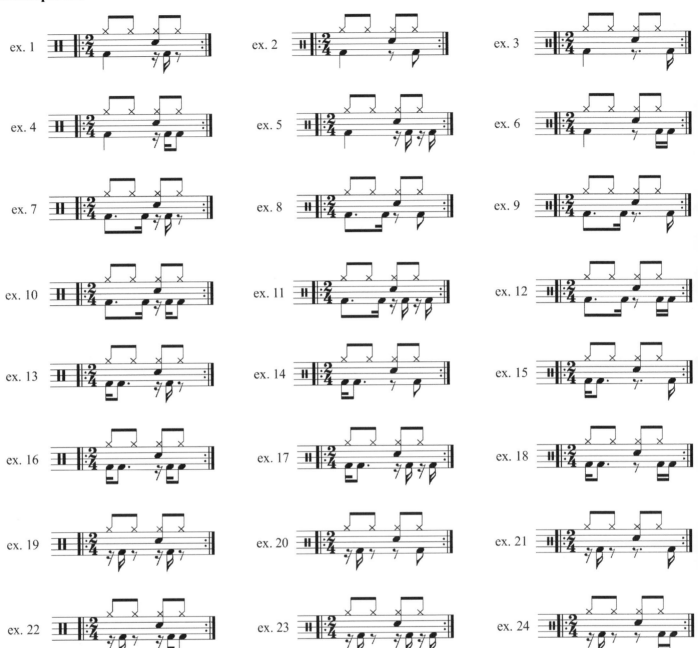

Lesson Two – Grip Variations, Accented Notes

Lesson Overview

Grip variations and *accented notes* are both important elements in the control of your sticks. This lesson will be an introduction to these concepts.

We will start by looking at the different grip variations, why they exist and their respective benefits.

Next, we will explore accented notes beginning with a comprehensive look at the theory, skills and techniques needed to play accents. Finally, we will work on some exercises that will cement them into your playing.

The subjects covered in this lesson will be invaluable throughout your musical life, so let's get started!

Grip Variations

Controlling the stick is at the heart of being a great drummer. Because of this, a variety of grip techniques and variations have been explored over the years. Each technique and variation was created to achieve a specific purpose and function. Some have amazing applications and have become ubiquitous throughout the drumming world. Others were abandoned as their functions were no longer needed. Here we will study the three main grip variations in modern drumming.

What are Grip Variations?

Grip variations are different from grip techniques. Grip techniques relate to *how* you hold the stick, while grip variations relate to *where* you hold and position the stick.

There are numerous different grip variations, but this section will concentrate on the three most commonly used. These are the *German grip*, *French grip* and the *American grip*. They get their names from the countries that used them in military marching bands.

Why Have Different Grip Variations?

Each variation offers different playing possibilities. They all produce different sounds and create a different feel to your playing. Certain drumming techniques favour particular variations because of the attributes associated with them (such as speed, strength, power or accuracy). After you have become used to these variations you will find that you will switch between them naturally, without thinking, when needed.

Grip variations are important to understand and study as they enhance your playing and allow you to express yourself on the drums.

This section examines the three most implemented variations of matched grip and explains their applications. However, there is no set rule for any drumming skill, technique or playing style. It is up to you to discover how you want to use these variations and how you want to implement them into your playing.

German Grip

The German grip's main function is to produce power and loud dynamics.

The German Grip's Main Attributes

- Palms facing down

- Sticks at 90 degrees

- Controlled mostly by the wrist

- Creates a lot of power

Constructing a German Grip

- Hold the sticks with a matched grip

- Place the palms of your hands parallel with the drum head and hold the sticks at about a 90-degree angle to each other

- The movement of the stick is mostly created by the wrist and helped by the fingers

The German grip is louder and more powerful because the movement is controlled by the muscles in the forearm which are larger and more powerful than the muscles in the fingers.

German Grip Movement Analysis

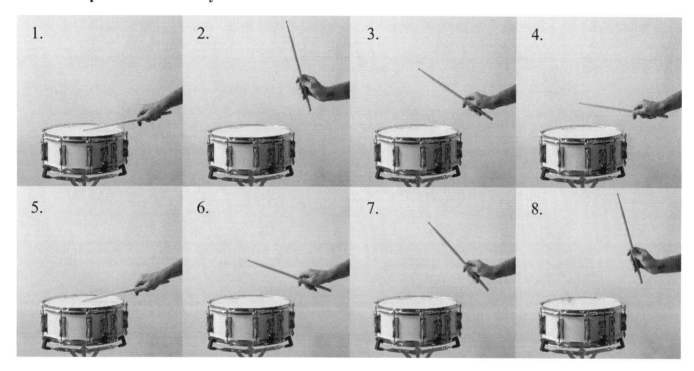

1. Start with the tip of the stick in the centre of the snare drum. Hold the sticks in the matched grip and have the palms of your hands facing down.

2. Bring the stick to about 90-degrees by bending your wrist and slightly relaxing the fingers.

3. Start to bring the tip of the stick to the centre of the snare drum by straightening your wrist and contracting your fingers.

4. Just before the stick hits the skin, the wrist is straight and the fingers are contracted.

5. As the stick hits the skin, the fingers relax to allow the stick to rebound.

6. As the stick rebounds back, the fingers start to control the rebound by guiding it back to 90-degrees.

7. As the fingers start to control the rebound of the stick, the wrist starts to bend.

8. As the stick reaches 90-degrees, the fingers have fully controlled the rebound and are back in their relaxed position. The wrist is bent and the whole process is ready to start again.

French Grip - (a.k.a. Timpani Grip)

The French grip's main function is to produce more articulate patterns and faster playing

The French Grip's Main Attributes

- Thumbs on top of the sticks

- Sticks at 40 degrees

- Controlled mostly by the fingers

- Creates more control

Constructing a French Grip

- Hold the sticks in matched grip

- Place the palms of your hands facing each other with your thumbs on top of the sticks

Traditionally, the sticks would be held parallel with each other, however this can be uncomfortable, so the typical angle of the sticks is about 40 degrees to each other.

The movement of the stick is mostly created by the fingers and helped by the wrist. This allows for more articulate and faster playing, as the muscles in the fingers are smaller and faster than the muscles in the forearm.

Movement Analysis of French Grip

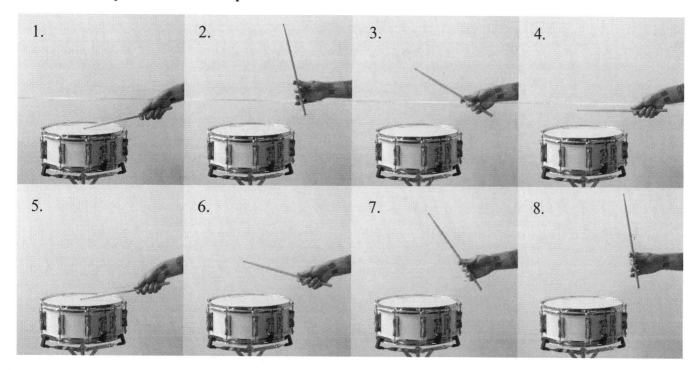

1. Start with the tip of the stick in the centre of the snare drum. Hold the sticks in the matched grip and have the palms of your hands facing each other with your thumbs on top of the stick.

2. Bring the stick to about 90-degrees by relaxing the fingers and slightly bending your wrist.

3. Start to bring the tip of the stick to the centre of the snare drum by contracting your fingers and straightening your wrist.

4. Just before the stick hits the skin, the fingers are contracted and the wrist is straight.

5. As the stick hits the skin, the fingers relax to allow the stick to rebound.

6. As the stick rebounds back, the fingers start to control the rebound by guiding it back to 90-degrees.

7. As the fingers start to control the rebound of the stick, the wrist starts to bend.

8. As the stick reaches 90-degrees, the fingers have fully controlled the rebound and are back in their relaxed position. The wrist is bent and the whole process is ready to start again.

American Grip – (a.k.a. Hybrid Grip)

The American grip is a general-purpose grip

American Grip's Main Attributes

- Hands halfway between German grip and French grip

- Sticks at 65 degrees

- Controlled by the fingers and wrist

Constructing the American Grip

The American grip is a hybrid of the French and German grips.

- Hold the sticks in matched grip

- Place the palms of your hands at a 45-degree angle (half way between French and German)

- Keep the angle of the sticks at about 65 degrees (half way between French and German)

The movement of the stick is created by both the fingers and the wrist. The American Grip is a general-purpose grip as it offers power and articulation, although the power created is not as strong as the German grip, and the articulation is not as great as the French grip.

Movement Analysis of American Grip

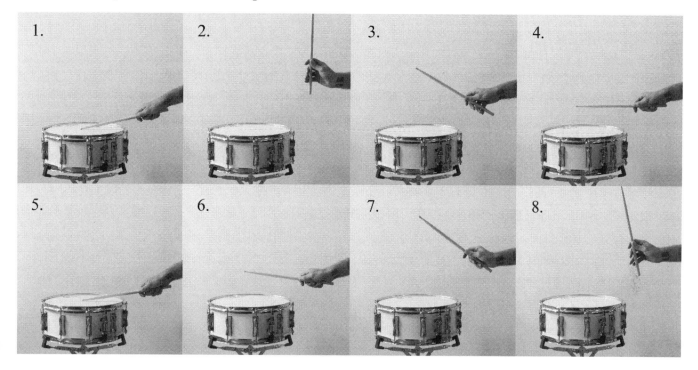

1. Start with the tip of the stick in the centre of the snare drum. Hold the sticks in the matched grip and have the palms of your hands facing each other with your thumbs on top of the stick.

2. Bring the stick to about 90-degrees by relaxing the fingers and slightly bending your wrist.

3. Start to bring the tip of the stick to the centre of the snare drum by contracting your fingers and straightening your wrist.

4. Just before the stick hits the skin, the fingers are contracted and the wrist is straight.

5. As the stick hits the skin, the fingers relax to allow the stick to rebound.

6. As the stick rebounds back, the fingers start to control the rebound by guiding it back to 90-degrees.

7. As the fingers start to control the rebound of the stick, the wrist starts to bend.

8. As the stick reaches 90-degrees, the fingers have fully controlled the rebound and are back in their relaxed position. The wrist is bent and the whole process is ready to start again.

Using Grip Variations

Below are ten exercises for practising the grip variations. Play each one using all three variations. Play each exercise until you are comfortable with it and gradually increase your speed using a metronome.

Tips

• Make sure your hand and stick placement are correct for each grip

• Concentrate on how your wrists and fingers work in different ways for each grip

• Pay attention to how the different variations affect your playing

Example 2a:

ex. 9

R R L L R R L L R R L L R R L L   R R L L R R L L R R L L R R L L

ex. 10

R R R R L L L L R R R R L L L L   R R R R L L L L R R R R L L L L

Accented Notes

Accented notes are a musical tool integral to good drum playing. Once you have learnt them and implemented them into your playing they will allow you to create very interesting and complicated rhythms that will take your drumming to the next level.

What are Accented Notes?

An accented note is simply a note that is played louder than a regular one. An accented note is played with more emphasis, with greater articulation and has a stronger attack. They're typically played about 50% louder than non-accented notes, but can be played at any volume.

Accented Note Notation

An accented note is indicated by an *accent mark* that is signified by a sideways V written directly above the note. An accent mark only affects the note it is written above. If multiple accents are required, then marks are written above every accented note.

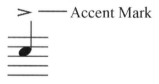

Here's an accented note played in conjunction with non-accented notes:

Here's a series of accented notes:

Full, Down, Tap and Up Strokes

Playing accents correctly and fluidly is not as simple as just playing them a bit louder. There are in fact four different *strokes* used to play accents proficiently. These strokes are called the *full* stroke, *down* stroke, *tap* stroke and *up* stroke. Mastery of them is essential to produce clear-sounding accents and patterns.

Each stroke has different attributes (the starting and finishing position of the stick) that affect the dynamic of the note and how the strike leads into the following one.

The starting position affects the dynamic of the note because a stroke with a higher starting position will create a louder dynamic.

The finishing position affects how the note leads into the following one because the finishing position of a stroke is the starting position of the next stroke.

By combining these strokes in different sequences, you can create accented patterns that sound great and are comfortable to play.

Full Stroke

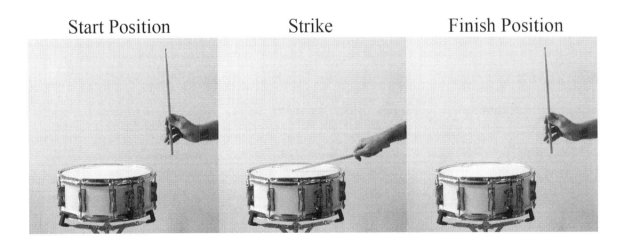

Starting Position:	The stick is at 90 degrees to the snare.
Finishing Position:	The stick is at 90 degrees to the snare.

The full stroke is played with a loud dynamic. It is used when one accented note is followed by another accented note.

It has a full range of movement and, because it finishes at 90 degrees, it must be followed by another accented note, such as another full stroke or down stroke.

Down Stroke

Start Position	Strike	Finish Position

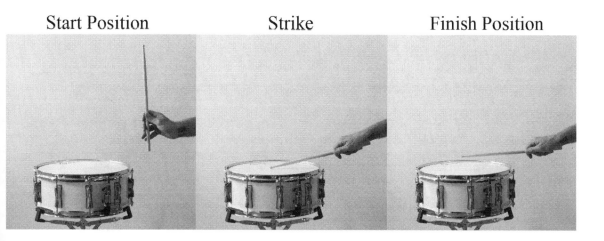

Starting Position:	The stick is at 90 degrees to the snare.
Finishing Position:	The stick is parallel to the skin with the tip 3-5cm away from the skin.

The down stroke is played with a loud dynamic. It is played when an accented note is followed by a non-accented note.

Because a down stroke finishes near the skin, it must be followed by non-accented note, such as a down stroke, tap stroke or up stroke.

Tap Stroke

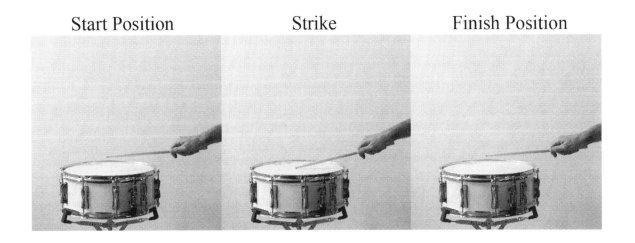

Starting Position:	The stick is parallel to the skin with the tip 3-5cm away from the skin.
Finishing Position:	The stick is parallel to the skin with the tip 3-5cm away from the skin.

The tap stroke is a non-accented note and is played with a low dynamic. It is played when a non-accented note is followed by another non-accented note.

Because a tap stroke starts and finishes near the skin, it must be followed by non-accented note, such as a tap stroke or up stroke.

Up Stroke

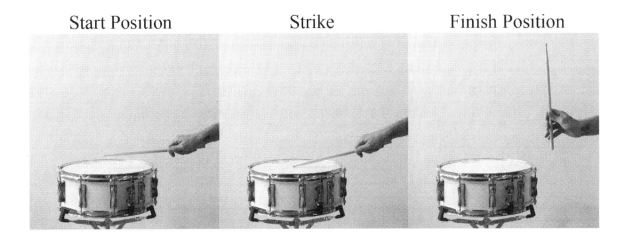

Starting Position:	The stick is parallel to the skin with the tip 3-5cm away from the skin.
Finishing Position:	The stick is at 90 degrees to the snare.

The up stroke is a non-accented note and is played with a low dynamic. It is played when a non-accented note is followed by an accented note. It has a full range of movement and, because it finishes at 90 degrees, it must be followed by an accented note, such as a full stroke or down stroke.

Playing the Strokes

The exercise below teaches you to practise the four strokes. Play the exercise continuously in full stroke until you are comfortable with it, then repeat it with down, tap and up strokes. Work with a metronome to make sure you're playing in time and gradually increase the speed.

Remember that these strokes are normally played in sequence, so they may feel unnatural when played in isolation.

Tips

- Ensure that the start and finish position of each stroke is correct

- Make sure that the accented strokes (full and down) have a loud dynamic and the non-accented notes have a low dynamic

- Play the exercise slowly

ex. 1

Single Hand Stroke Sequences

Now you're used to playing the four strokes on their own, it's time to start playing them in sequence. Below are four exercises that teach you single hand stroke sequences They will help you learn how the different strokes correspond with the accent marks and each other.

Play each exercise first with the right hand, then the left.

Above each note is a letter that shows which stroke is being played.

F = Full Stroke

D = Down Stroke

T = Tap Stroke

U = Up Stroke

These letters are for learning purposes only and won't be written anywhere else.

Tips

• Pay attention to how each stroke relates to the accents played

• Ensure that the start and finish position of each stroke is correct, as this creates the fluid motion into the next note

• Make sure that the accented notes (full and down) are loud and the non-accented notes (tap and up) are quiet. There must be a clear difference in sound between accented and non-accented notes.

• Play the exercise slowly.

Example 2b:

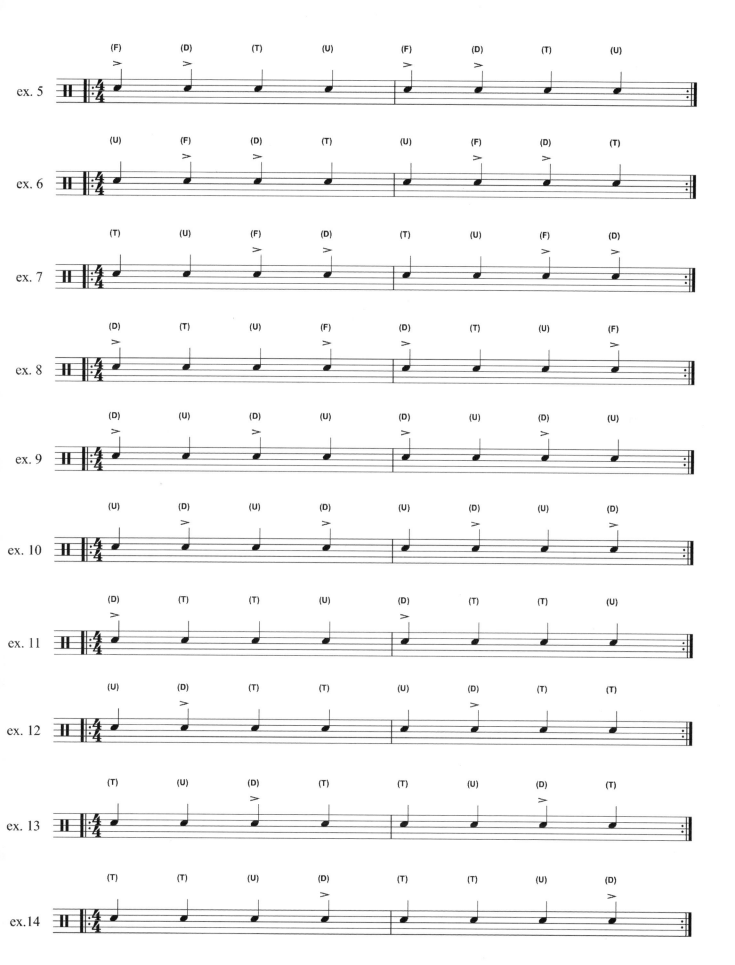

35

Single Hand Stroke Sequences

Two Voice Playing

Playing accents with the hands while keeping time on the bass drum is a common occurrence in drumming and is taught in the next set of exercises. Ensure that the accents in the hands do not affect the dynamics of the bass drum. Learn each exercise first with the right hand, then with the left hand.

Tips

- Ensure that the start and finish position of each stroke is correct as this creates the fluid motion into the next note

- Ensure there is a clear difference in dynamic between accented and non-accented notes

- Ensure that the unisons between the snare drum and the bass drum are together

- Be careful that playing the bass drum does not affect the dynamics on the snare drum

Example 2c:

Lesson Three – Accents on Two Hands

Lesson Overview

In lesson three we will study accents in a greater depth and focus on playing them in two hands. This is a far more natural way of playing accents, as most rhythms played on a drum kit are performed like this.

Playing accents with two hands requires more dexterity, but don't let this deter you as these exercises will leave you able to play any accented rhythm with ease.

Two Hand Stroke Sequences

In the previous lesson you studied accents, the four strokes needed to play them and single hand stroke sequences. However, accented rhythms are usually played on two hands. In this section you will learn to perform *two hand stroke sequences*.

Two hand stroke sequences may seem complicated at first, but they rely on the same techniques as their single hand equivalents.

I have written 24 exercises that will help you perfect your two hand stroke sequences. Practise each exercise until you can play it in time with a slow metronome.

Tips

- Pay attention to the sticking and use the correct stroke for the correct hand

- Ensure that the start and finish position of each stroke is correct to create a fluid motion into the next note on that hand

- Keep a clear difference in dynamics between accented and non-accented notes

Example 3a:

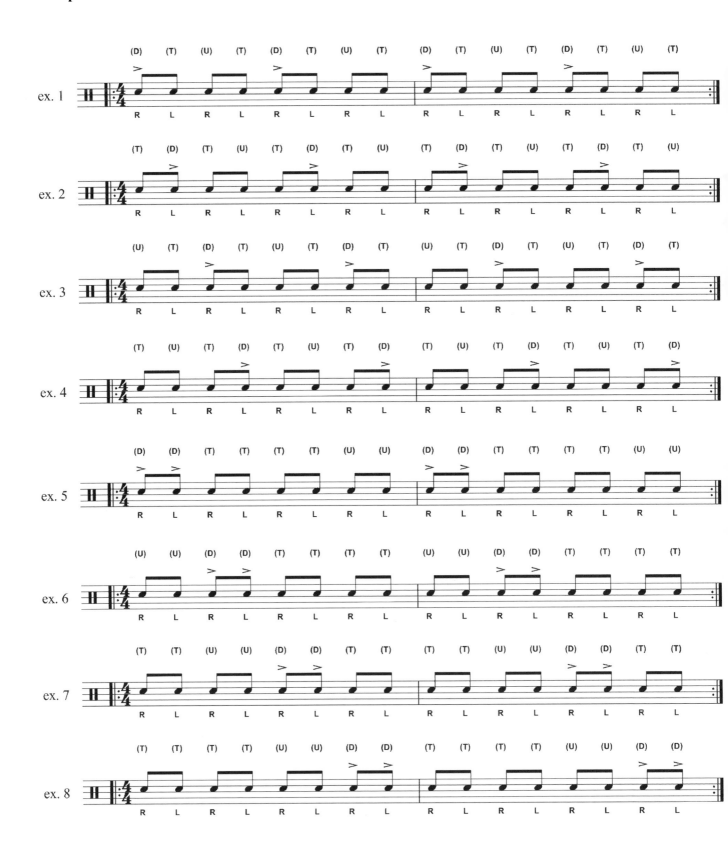

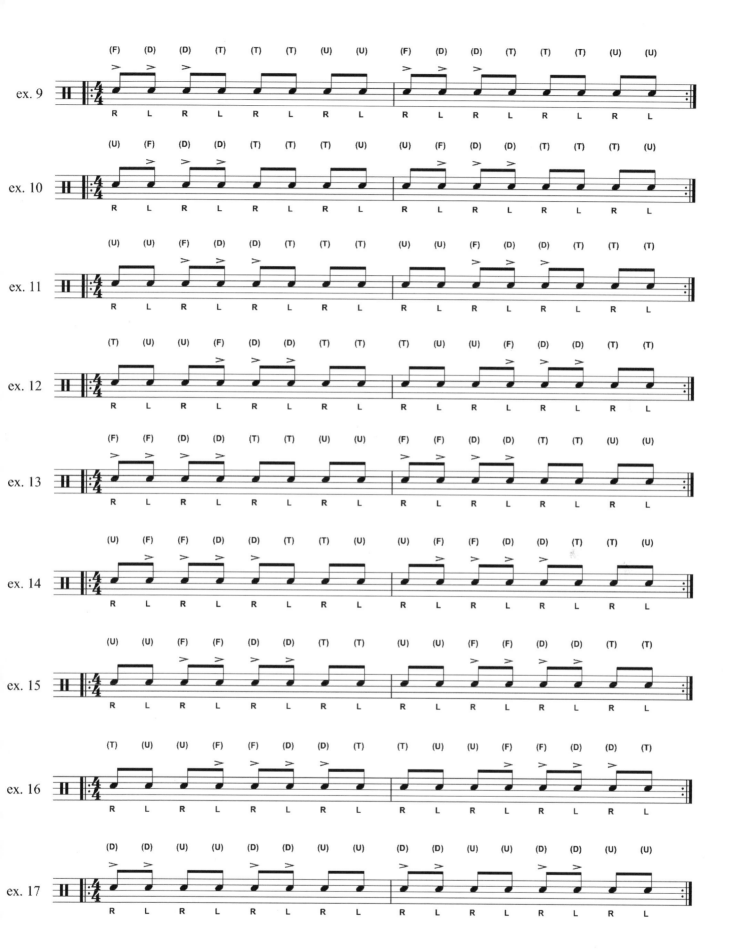

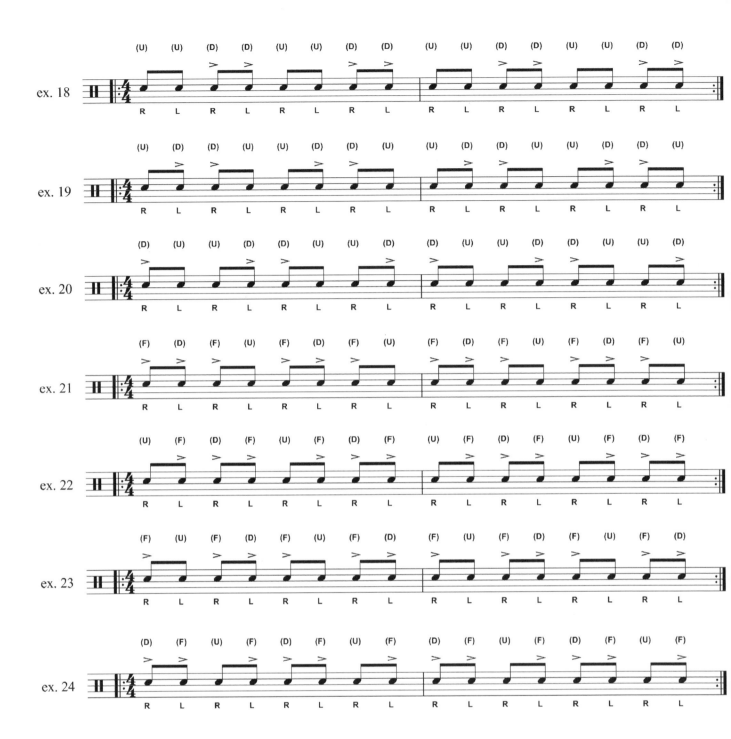

ex. 18

ex. 19

ex. 20

ex. 21

ex. 22

ex. 23

ex. 24

42

Two Hand Stroke Sequences
Two Voice Playing

Much like the single hand stroke sequences, it is important to be able to play two hand stroke sequences while keeping time on the bass drum. In the following exercises you will play different two hand stroke sequences and constant 1/4 notes on the bass drum.

Tips

- Pay attention to the sticking

- Make sure you are using the correct stroke for the correct hand

- Ensure that the start and finish position of each stroke is correct

- Concentrate on your dynamics. Ensure that playing the bass drum does not affect the dynamics of the snare drum

- Ensure that the unisons between the snare drum and the bass drum are together

Example 3b:

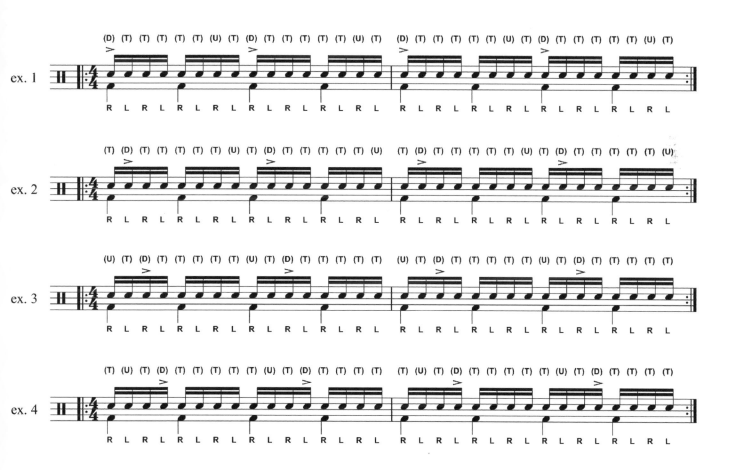

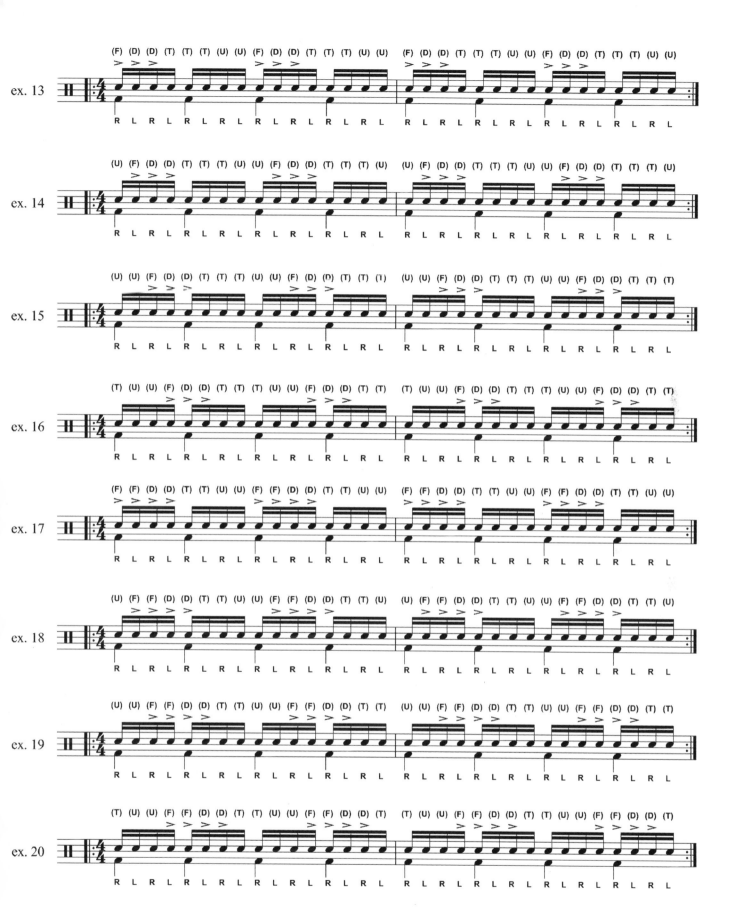

Two Hand Stroke Sequence with Multiple Notes

Accents occur in all aspects of drumming, so it's important to understand how to play accents when performing various sequences of notes. Even if there is a gap between strokes, it is imperative that you perform the full movement of each stroke to prepare for the next note.

Tips

- Make sure you are using the correct stroke for the correct hand

- Ensure that the start and finish position of each stroke is correct

- Concentrate on your dynamics. Ensure that playing the bass drum does not affect the dynamics of the snare drum

Example 3c:

Lesson Four – Displaced Backbeats

Lesson overview

This lesson will develop your groove playing by teaching you the concept of displaced backbeats. The exercises will evolve into more musical and complex playing examples that show how these ideas are used in regular playing.

Displaced backbeats are an essential concept to understand. They give your groove playing extra depth, they sound awesome and they are incredibly fun to play.

Let's get stuck in!

Displaced Backbeats

Displaced backbeats create a form of *tension and release* that can dramatically affect the feel of a groove. A *backbeat* (as you learnt in volume one) is the rhythmic accent on the second and fourth beat in a bar. A *displaced* backbeat simply moves the position of the backbeat, and is typically done by moving it an 1/8th note.

There are two types of displacement which can be used.

Delayed displacement is playing the backbeat *after* where it would typically occur.

Forward displacement is playing the backbeat *before* where it would typically occur.

Each of these techniques adds a different feel to the groove and allows you to create more sophisticated rhythms.

Below, you will first see the regular backbeat position followed by the two forms of displaced backbeat.

Only the backbeat on beat 4 has been displaced, but it can be done on the second beat too.

Displaced Backbeat Grooves

Displaced Backbeats with 1/8th Note Bass Drum

Let's start by playing some displaced backbeats.

Below are 34 exercises that will teach you how to play displaced backbeats musically. Each one contains an 1/8th note hi-hat and bass drum, and introduces different displaced backbeats.

Playing displaced backbeats can feel unnatural at first, but the more you play them the more they will become a confident and integral part of your playing.

Learn each exercise with a metronome and, as your confidence increases, slowly begin to increase the tempo.

Tips

- Ensure the unisons between the snare and the hi-hat are together

- Do not rush or slow down when playing the displaced backbeat

Delayed Displaced Backbeats

Example 4a:

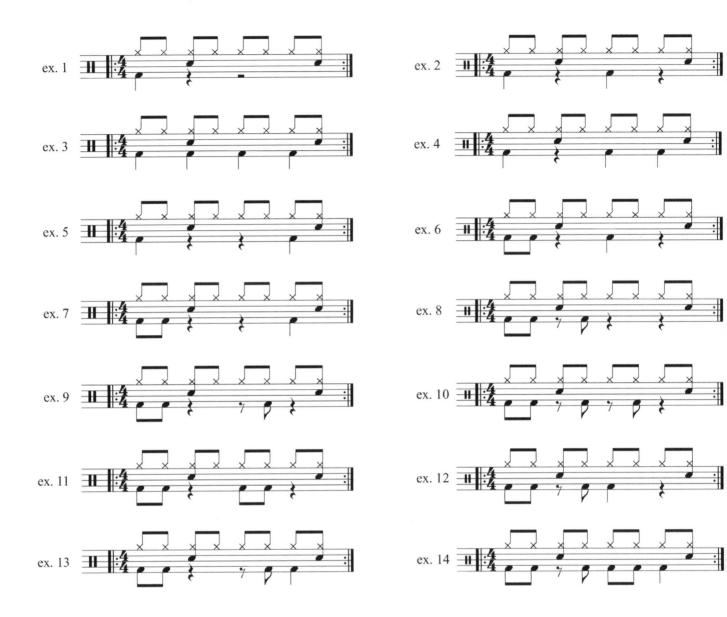

Forward Displaced Backbeats

Example 4b:

Displaced Backbeat Grooves

Displaced Backbeats with 1/16th Note Bass Drum

Now that you have gained confidence with displaced backbeats and 1/8th note bass drum rhythms, it's time to increase the challenge by learning some displaced backbeats with 1/16th note bass drum rhythms.

Each exercise contains a constant hi-hat pattern, 1/16th note bass drum rhythm, and displaced backbeats.

Tips

• Make sure that the unisons between the snare and the hi-hat are together

• Do not rush or slow down when playing the displaced backbeat

• Pay attention to where the displaced backbeat is and the rhythms that surround it

• Ensure the bass drum pattern does not affect the displaced backbeat placement

Learn each exercise with a metronome and, as your confidence increases, slowly begin to increase the tempo.

Forward Displaced Backbeats

Example 4c:

Delayed Displaced Backbeats

Example 4d:

Displaced Backbeat Combined with Regular Backbeats

Displaced backbeat grooves are not typically used as part of a continuous groove as they can sound overpowering. They are more commonly used as an inflection in a groove with a regular backbeat. Think of the displaced backbeat as a fill that creates some tension that doesn't overshadow the groove.

The following exercises are divided into two-bar and four-bar phrases with a mixture of delayed and forward displacement.

Learn each exercise with a metronome and, as your confidence increases, slowly begin to increase the tempo.

Tips

- Read the exercises before playing and work out where the displaced backbeat is

- Do not rush or slow down when playing the displaced backbeat

- Ensure the bass drum pattern does not affect the displaced backbeat placement

Two-Bar Grooves

Example 4e:

Four-Bar Phrasing

Example 4f:

Lesson Five – Dynamics

Lesson Overview

This lesson focuses more on dynamics. We'll take an in-depth look at the notation, theory and skills needed before moving into some musical exercises that teach you to play them and help you get used to how they feel.

Dynamics make music and grooves come alive and are constantly used in all drum playing. Mastering them will allow you to play with greater articulation and give you better control over your musical expression.

Let's get going!

Dynamic Notation

Dynamic marks are a musical symbol used to indicate the volume at which to play. These symbols are usually written underneath the stave, but you'll see them placed wherever is the clearest to read.

Dynamic marks indicate that the music must be played at that volume from where the mark is written until you see the next one.

This table shows you each dynamic symbol, along with its name and description.

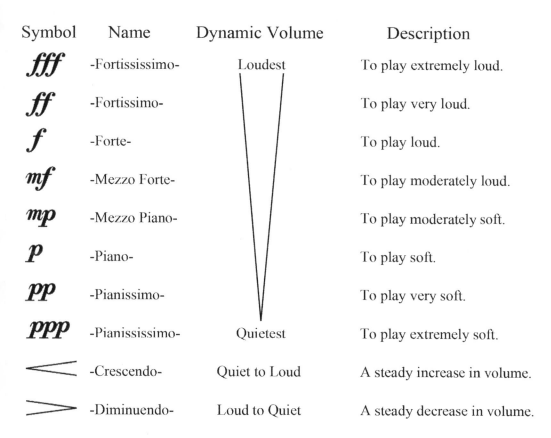

Symbol	Name	Dynamic Volume	Description
fff	-Fortississimo-	Loudest	To play extremely loud.
ff	-Fortissimo-		To play very loud.
f	-Forte-		To play loud.
mf	-Mezzo Forte-		To play moderately loud.
mp	-Mezzo Piano-		To play moderately soft.
p	-Piano-		To play soft.
pp	-Pianissimo-		To play very soft.
ppp	-Pianississimo-	Quietest	To play extremely soft.
<	-Crescendo-	Quiet to Loud	A steady increase in volume.
>	-Diminuendo-	Loud to Quiet	A steady decrease in volume.

The four most common dynamics are Forte (f), Mezzo Forte (mf), Mezzo Piano (mp) and Piano (p).

How to Play Different Dynamics

Let's learn how to create these different dynamics. In previous lessons we have studied grip techniques, strokes and foot techniques. Good dynamic playing utilizes all these skills.

When playing in *fortississimo* (the loudest dynamic) you should use the powerful *full stroke*.

When playing in *pianississimo* (the quietest dynamic) you should use the gentle *tap stroke*.

When playing the dynamics in between fortississimo and pianississimo you should use varying levels of power and strokes of different heights to achieve to dynamic you want.

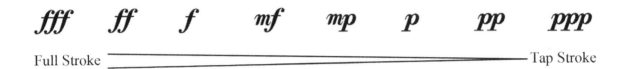

There is no set rule for which grip to use, as fortississimo and pianississimo can be played with either the German, French or American grip. However, the German grip has naturally loud dynamics, making it easier to play fortississimo. The French grip offers more control, making it easier to play pianississimo.

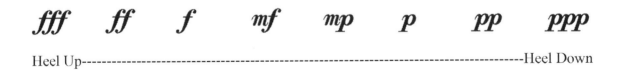

Playing Different Dynamics on the Feet

When playing dynamics on the feet you should use the heel up technique for loud dynamics as it is impossible to create loud dynamics with heel down technique.

When playing quiet dynamics, it's up to you to decide which technique to use, as it is possible to play quiet dynamics with both. However, it is generally easier to play the quiet dynamics with heel down.

fff   ff   f   mf   mp   p   pp   ppp

Heel Up--Heel Down

Playing Dynamics

Now that you understand how dynamics are written and what they mean, it is time to start playing them.

Below are a series of exercises for practising dynamic playing. Each exercise has the same rhythm – what changes is the volume. Repeat Example 5a four times at each dynamic. Begin at the quietest dynamic marking (ppp), and then gradually increase to maximum volume (fff). Listen to the audio to help you move through the dynamics, ppp, pp, p, m, mf, f, ff, fff.

Tips

- Ensure there is a clear difference in volume between each dynamic

- Ensure you have correct body posture, arm movement and stroke technique

Example 5a:

ex. 1

ppp

Dynamics on Two Voices

Dynamics are not just played on the hands, but also on the feet. The following exercises allow you to practise two-voice dynamics.

Tips

- Pay attention to the dynamic markings

- Work out what each dynamic mark means before playing

- Ensure there is a clear difference in volume between each dynamic

- Ensure you have correct body posture, arm movement and stroke technique

Example 5b:

Dynamic Changes

It's important to understand how to switch from one dynamic to another as this is an important part of playing music. The following exercises will teach you this skill.

Tips

- Pay attention to the dynamic marks and work out what each one means before playing

- Ensure there is a clear difference in volume between each dynamic

Example 5c:

Crescendo and Diminuendo

Crescendos and *diminuendos* have a lot of applications and are often used to lead from one dynamic to another. They can be used to end a musical phrase, as part of a fill, or as a musical build or fade out.

Crescendo

A crescendo is a steady increase from a quiet to a loud dynamic. It can be as short as a few notes or can be as long as several bars.

begin crescendo here   end crescendo here

Diminuendo (a.k.a. decrescendo)

A diminuendo is a steady decrease from a loud to a quiet dynamic. It can be as short as a few notes or as long as several bars.

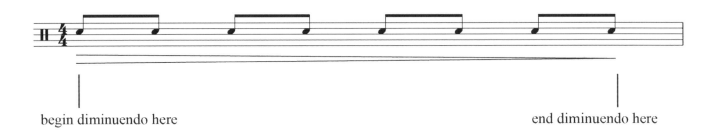

begin diminuendo here   end diminuendo here

What dynamics to play

A crescendo normally starts at piano (p) and finishes at forte (f).

A diminuendo normally start at forte (f) and finishes at piano (p).

However, the dynamic volume of crescendos and diminuendos are open to interpretation, as they are relative to the volume of the music. For example, a crescendo in a particularly loud piece of music will have a louder starting and finishing dynamic then a crescendo in a quiet piece of music. Most of the time is it up to the performer to work out what levels are needed.

Crescendos often begin at a quieter volume to the music being played and finish louder. A diminuendo often begins at a louder volume and finishes at a quieter one.

Playing Crescendos and Diminuendos

Now you understand the concept of crescendos and diminuendos it is time to start playing them.

Play the crescendos in the following examples from piano to forte, and play the diminuendos from forte to piano.

Tips

•   Pay attention to the dynamic marks. Look at where they start and where they end

•   Work out what each dynamic mark means before playing

•   Ensure that crescendos have a steady increase in volume, and that diminuendos have a steady decrease in volume

•   Be careful not to speed up as you get louder or slow down when you get quieter

Example 5d:

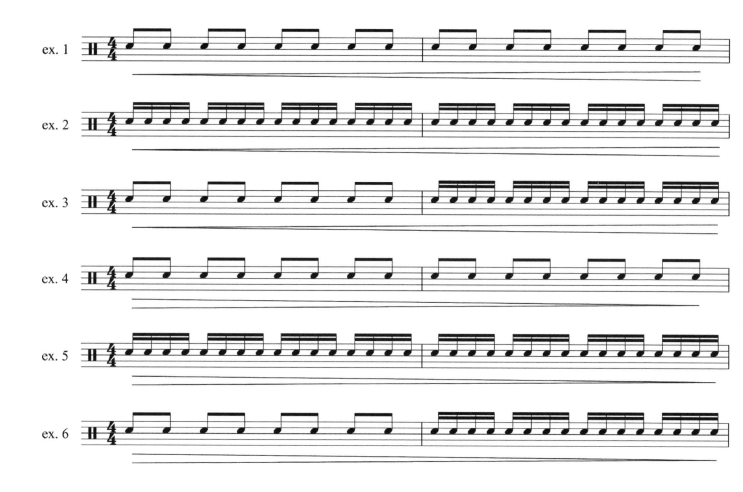

Applied Crescendos and Diminuendos

Crescendos and diminuendos are, of course, normally played within a piece of music, so it's important to learn how to play them in sequence with other dynamics. Below are eight exercises for practising this skill.

Tips

- Pay attention to the suggested dynamics

- Ensure that crescendos have a steady increase in volume, and that diminuendos have a steady decrease in volume

Example 5e:

Lesson Six – Ghost Notes

Lesson Overview

In this lesson we will study the reverse of an accent: a *ghost note*. A ghost note is a note with a much lower volume to the rest of the phrase.

Ghost notes are a great musical tool for drummers and can be tough to play at first. However, you'll soon find that they add a whole new dimension to your playing.

Let's start!

Ghost Notes

Ghost Notes are one of the cooler tools in a drummer's arsenal. They add subtlety to a rhythm without taking attention away from the main groove. They add an extra dimension to the music and can turn a standard groove into something far more rhythmically interesting.

Ghost notes are typically played on a 1/16th note subdivision to give the groove a subtle 1/16th note rhythmic feel. This can make the groove sound fuller without being overpowering.

The name "ghost note" can be misleading as it should be heard, albeit very quietly. A more appropriate term would be an *anti-accent*.

Ghost Note Dynamics

A ghost note is typically played around 50% quieter than a regular one, however they can be played at any level as long as they are quieter than the main pulse.

Ghost Note Notation

A ghost note is indicated by parenthesis (brackets) around a note head. If multiple ghost notes are required, then parentheses must be written around every desired note.

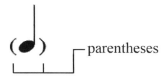

Here's a ghost note played in conjunction with regular notes:

And here's a series of ghost motes:

Ghost Note Playing

Now that you understand how to read ghost notes, it is time to start playing them.

A ghost note is typically played with a tap stroke. In the following examples, use a tap stroke to play the ghost notes and a non-accented full stroke to play the regular notes.

As always, use a metronome to gauge and increase your speed.

Tips

- Work out where the ghost notes are before playing

- Ensure there is a clear difference in volume between ghost notes and regular notes

- Play the ghost notes 50% quieter than the regular ones

Example 6a:

Ghost Notes in Conjunction with Backbeat

As the backbeat is one of the most integral parts of a groove, you must learn how to play ghost notes in conjunction with the snare.

Tips

*   Work out where the ghost notes are before playing

*   Make sure that the ghost notes are about 50% quieter than the regular notes

*   Make certain there is a clear difference in volume between the backbeat and the ghost notes

Example 6b:

Grooves with one ghost note

Grooves with two ghost notes

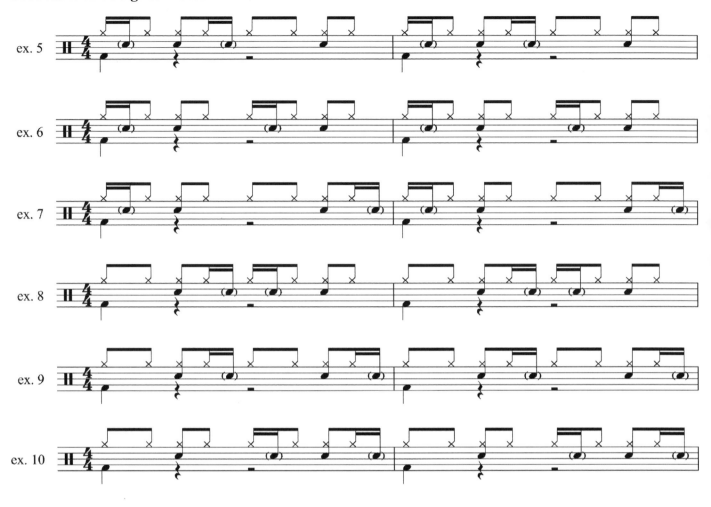

Grooves with three ghost notes

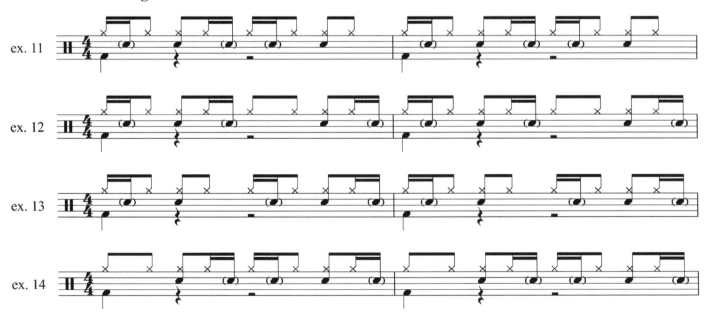

A groove with four ghost notes

ex. 15

Ghost Notes with 1/8th Note Bass Drums Patterns

Now that you are getting comfortable with ghost notes in a groove, it's time to integrate them into more complex 1/8th note groove ideas.

Each exercise below is divided into four parts (a, b, c and d). Each part contains the same groove with a different ghost note pattern. The difficulty increases as you move through the parts.

Tips

• Work out where the ghost notes are before playing the exercises

• Do not let the ghost note pattern affect how you play the bass drum pattern, and vice versa

Example 6c:

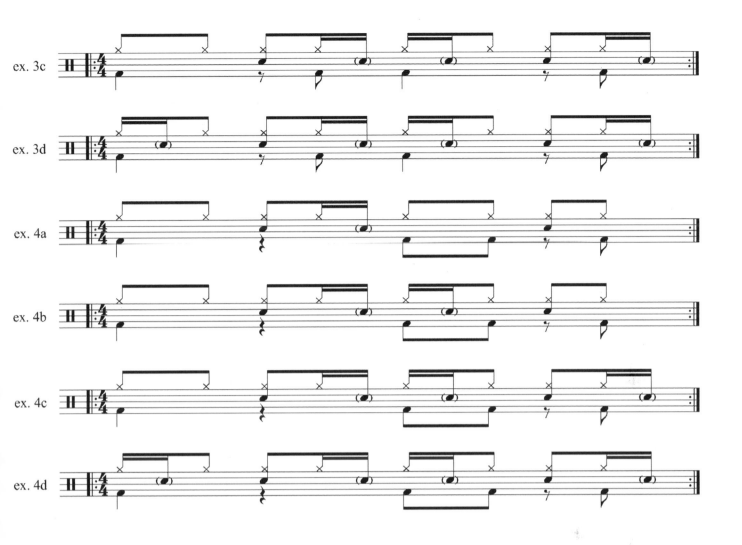

These exercises can be applied to any bass drum pattern, so try them with some 1/16th note patterns from earlier in the book.

Lesson Seven – Triplets

Lesson Overview

So far, we have looked at rhythms that can be divided easily into two: whole notes, 1/2 notes, 1/4 notes, 1/8th notes and 1/16th notes. But what happens if we want to divide a beat into three? That's where the *triplet* comes in.

In this lesson we will explore many triplet-based rhythms and learn many cool musical applications.

Triplet Introduction

Triplets are a very common rhythm that changes the feeling of a piece of music. They are an essential skill to master as many genres (such as jazz, blues and swing) are based on them. They can be challenging to play correctly at first, but they add a new dimension of possibilities to your grooves.

What are Tuplets?

Tuplets are subdivisions of notes that don't fit nicely into groups of two. Normally, every note can be divided into two to create another note. For example, a 1/4 note divided by two creates an 1/8th note. However, what if you want to divide a note into 3, 5, 6 or 7 etc?

There are many types of tuplets in music. Each one indicates the number of subdivisions within a note. The different types are:

Triplet (3 subdivisions)

Quintuplet (5 subdivisions)

Sextuplet (6 subdivisions)

Septuplet (7 subdivisions)

Nonuplet (9 subdivisions)

Decuplet (10 subdivisions).

Some of these tuplets are very rarely used, such as nonuplets and decuplets, but the triplet is extremely common.

Triplets

What is a Triplet?

A triplet is a grouping of three evenly spaced notes played in the time of two notes. For example, an 1/8th note triplet is played in the same amount of time as two 1/8th notes.

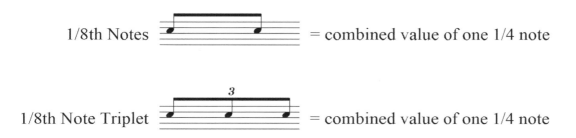

In the diagram below you can see how the values of 1/4 notes, 1/8th notes, and 1/8th note triplets coincide with each other.

Triplet Notation

Triplets are written with a "3" above the centre of the grouping.

Triplet Values

The most common triplet values are 1/2 note triplets, 1/4 note triplets, 1/8th note triplets and 1/16th note triplets. They're all shown in the diagram below.

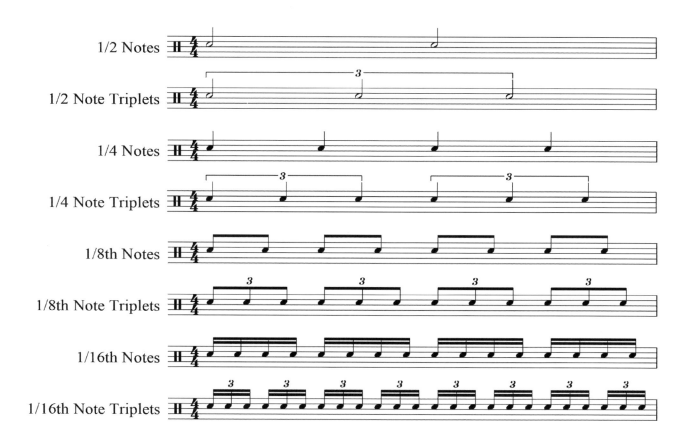

1/8th Note Triplets

The 1/8th note triplet is the most commonly used of all the tuplets.

1/8th Note Triplet Count

Like all other notes, triplets have a count.

To count a triplet, say out loud,

"1-trip-let-2-trip-let-3-trip-let-4-trip-let…"

The 1, 2, 3, 4 are on the 1/4 note pulse. The "trip" is on the second division and the "let" is on the third division.

| 1 | trip | let | 2 | trip | let | 3 | trip | let | 4 | trip | let |

Here is the 1/8th note triplet count in reference to a 1/4 note count and an 1/8th note count.

1/4 note count	- 1			2			3			4		
1/8th note count	- 1	+		2	+		3	+		4	+	
1/8th note triplet count	- 1	trip	let	2	trip	let	3	trip	let	4	trip	let

It is imperative that triplets are evenly spaced as each note has equal value.

Triplet Stickings

Now that you understand the concept and theory of triplets, it is time to start playing them. The exercises below will teach you to play 1/8th note triplet rhythms.

Each exercise is a 1/8th note triplet rhythm with different sticking patterns. Play through each one with the indicated sticking until you are comfortable with it and then begin to speed it up with a metronome.

Tips

• Say the count out loud whilst playing the exercises

• Keep the notes evenly spaced

• Read the stickings before playing

Example 7a:

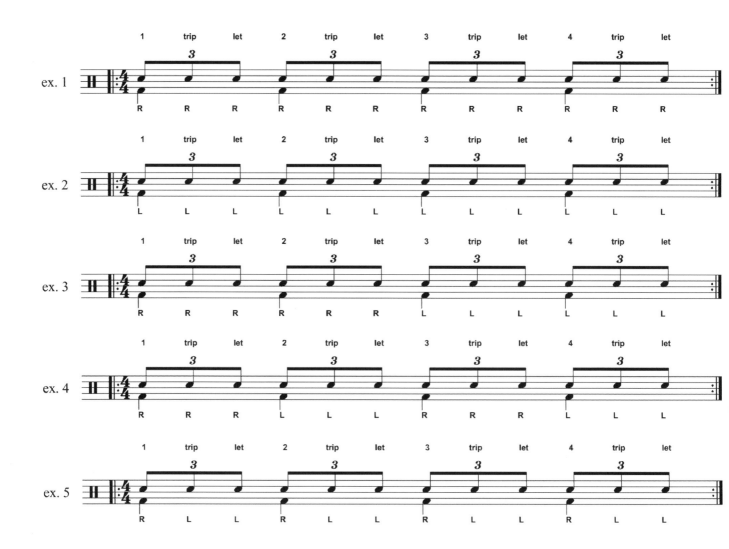

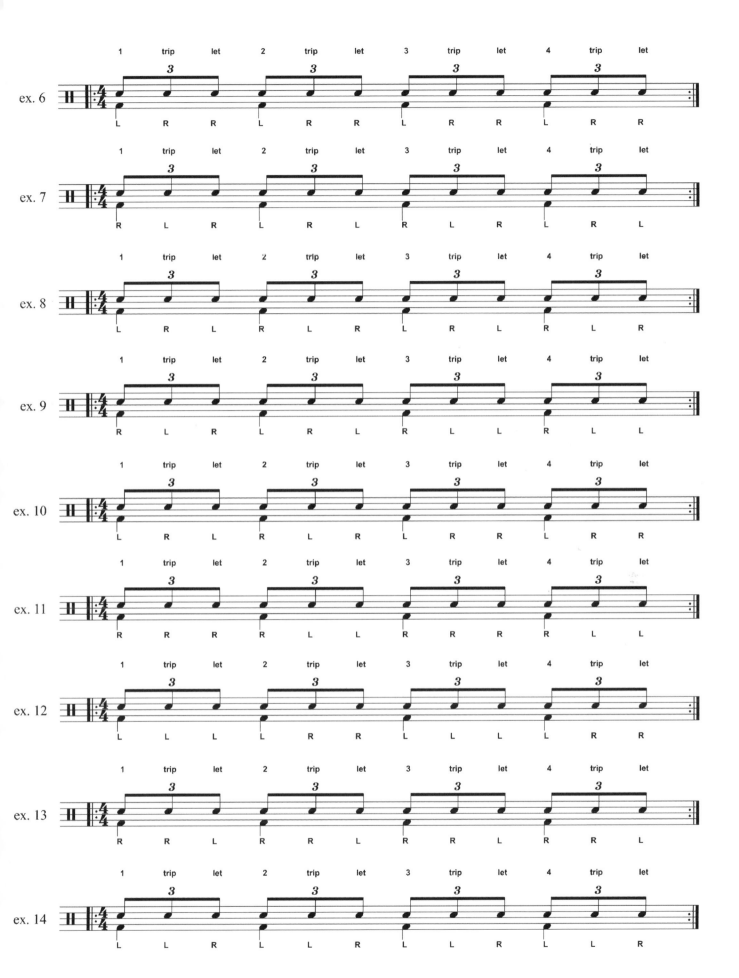

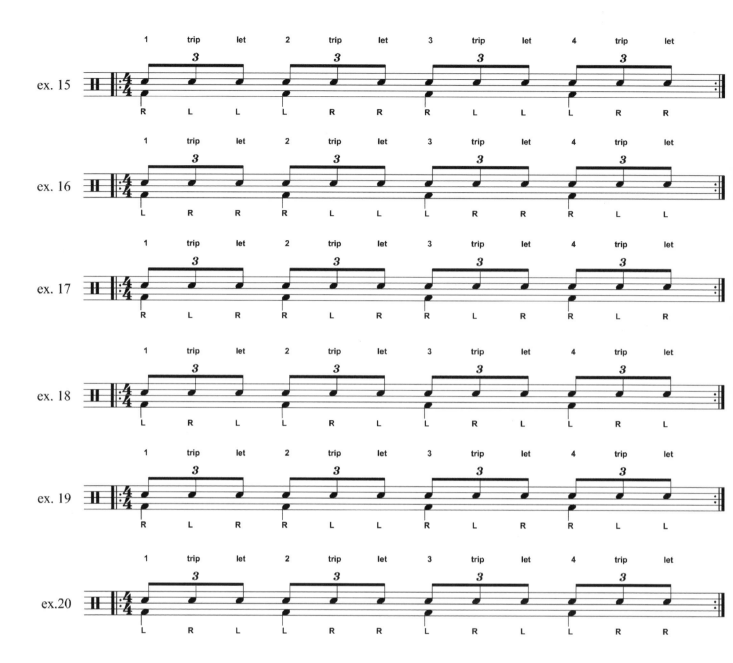

Triplets in Conjunction with Other Notes

Below are some exercises that will teach you to combine 1/8th note triplets with other note durations. Each exercise has a constant 1/4 note pulse on the bass drum to help you keep time and learn how the different rhythms coincide.

The transitions from even divisions to triplets can be difficult at first, as you learn to transition from odd- to even-note groupings.

Play through each exercise with the indicated sticking and work with a metronome to build confidence and speed.

Tips

- Work out the rhythms before playing

- Read the stickings before playing them

- Concentrate on the transitions between the triplets and the other notes

- Say the count out loud whilst playing

- Do not slow down or speed the tempo when transitioning into triplets

- Keep the bass drum strong and accurate. This will help you keep time

Example 7b:

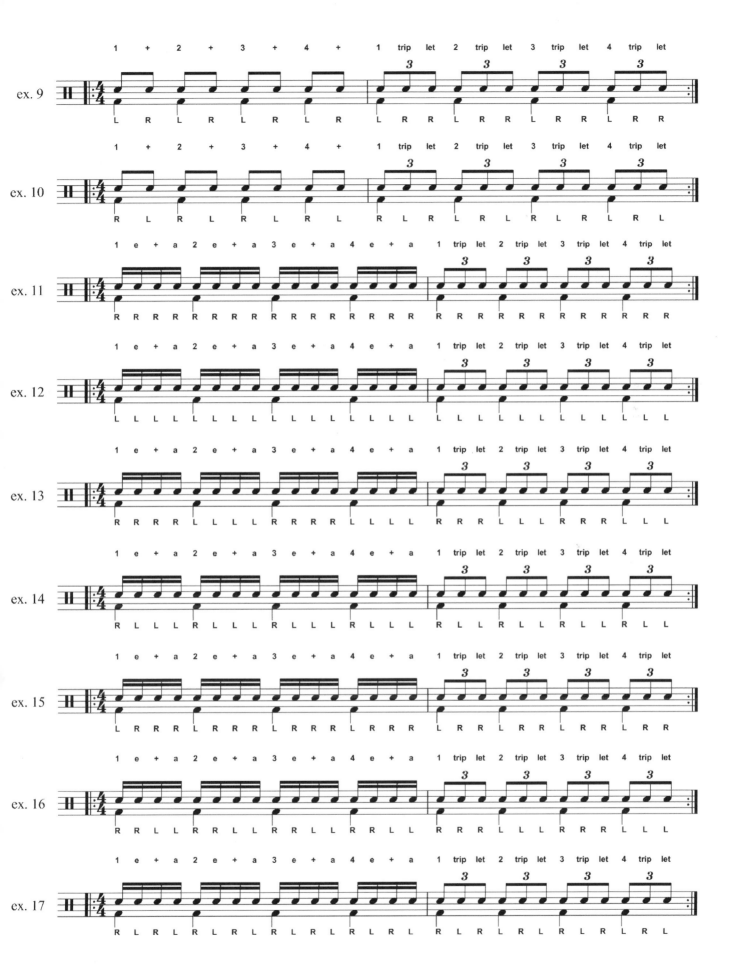

ex. 18

Now you are used to combining triplets with other notes, it is time to increase the difficulty level.

Each exercise will be an amalgamation of notes and rhythms and is written with two sticking patterns. Play each exercise with each sticking pattern until you are comfortable with it.

Tips

- Work out the rhythms before playing

- Read the stickings before playing them

- Concentrate on the transitions between the triplets and the other notes

- Do not slow down or speed the tempo when transitioning into triplets

- Keep the bass drum strong and accurate. This will help you keep time

Example 7c:

Lesson Eight – Open Hi-Hat Playing

Lesson Overview

This lesson focuses on the great technique of open hi-hat playing (opening and closing the hi-hats) and the necessary skills that support it. We first will explore its application, history, notation and techniques. Then we'll learn some great-sounding techniques, so that you get used to the movements, coordination and dexterity needed. Finally, we will look at some exercises that will get you playing some musical open hi-hat grooves.

Open hi-hat playing is a great tool to master, with many musical possibilities, so let's jump in!

Open Hi-Hat Playing Introduction

Open hi-hat playing is a fantastic technique that adds an extra dynamic layer in groove playing. The name open hi-hat playing refers to the act of opening and closing the hi-hat while playing a pattern on it. This allows you to create more sounds and produce more complex grooves and rhythms.

The concept of open hi-hat playing was developed soon after the hi-hat was created, as drummers and percussionists quickly realized its potential. It was heavily adopted in jazz, and still remains an integral part of jazz drumming. However, open hi-hat playing gained true notoriety when the early funk drummers started using it in their grooves. Drummers began to push the boundaries of what was possible. Now open hi-hat playing has been adopted into almost all styles of playing.

This technique does require a high degree of dexterity and coordination, but don't let this discourage you, as open hi-hat playing is a great skill to master and is lots of fun to play.

What is Open Hi-Hat Playing?

When a closed hi-hat is hit with a stick, it produces a very tight sound with sharp properties.

When an open hi-hat is hit with a stick, it produces a warmer, washy sound with richer resonance and more depth.

Hi-Hat Notation

An O indicates an open hi-hat (pedal open).

A + indicates a closed hi-hat (pedal closed).

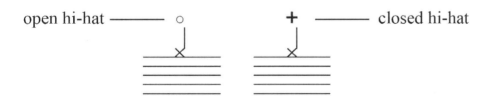

Here is an example of how this would be notated:

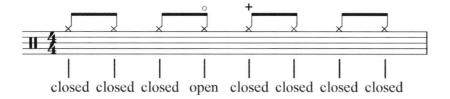

closed closed closed open closed closed closed closed

Sometimes multiple open hi-hats are played in a row. This does not require notating multiple "O"s, just one at the start of the open hi-hats and a + when they close again.

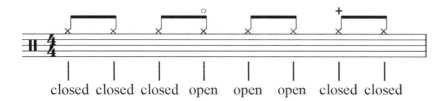

closed closed closed open open open closed closed

What stick position to use?

When playing closed hi-hats the tip of the stick plays on the surface of the hi-hat.

When playing open hi-hats the shoulder of the stick plays on the edge of the hi-hat.

stick position for playing closed hi-hat

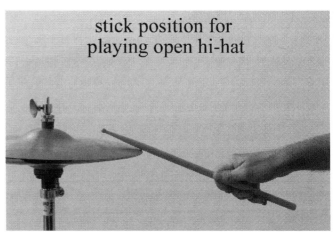

stick position for playing open hi-hat

There are no specific stick positions required for playing open hi-hats, so it's up to you to decide how you want to play it. Each stick position (studied in volume one) will affect the sound.

Heel Up or Heel Down?

While you can use heel up or heel down, open hi-hats are generally played with the heel down because it allows you to have greater control of the sound and gives you better balance.

How Far to Open the Hi-Hats?

The normal amount to open the hi-hats is about half an inch (1cm) and how far you open them will affect the sound that is produced.

For example, if the hi-hats are only opened by 1/16th of an inch (1mm) they will produce a rich sound with washy properties as the two cymbals have more contact with each other and will rattle more.

If the hi-hats are opened very wide, the cymbals will not have as much contact and will produce a different sound.

Playing Open Hi-Hats

Now it's time to start playing some open hi-hat patterns. The exercises isolate the hi-hats, so you get used to playing them without having to worry about anything else.

Tips

- Read through each exercise before playing

- Work out where the open hi-hats are and where you have to close them before playing

- Make sure the hi-hats are opened and closed on the correct notes

- Focus on your chosen stick position

- Pay attention to how much you are opening the hi-hat. Ensure it is the same every time

Example 8a:

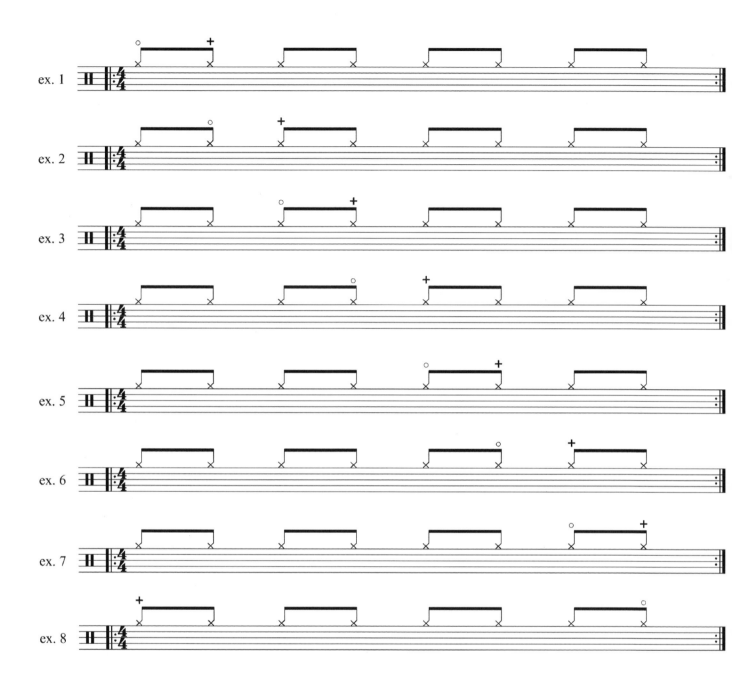

Two Voice Playing with Open Hi-Hats

Now let's get used to playing these patterns in coordination with your other limbs. Playing open hi-hats in conjunction with other voices requires a new level of dexterity and limb control and the exercises below will help you achieve this.

Each exercise is played on two voices: the first four are on the hi-hat and snare, and the second four are on the hi-hat and bass drum.

Tips

- Read through each exercise first and work out how the open hi-hats relate to the other instruments

- Play each exercise slowly, until you are comfortable with it

- The rhythms on the snare and bass should flow with the open hi-hat rhythms. Make sure they are not negatively affecting each other

Example 8b:

ex. 1

ex. 2

ex. 3

ex. 4

ex. 5

ex. 6

ex. 7

ex. 8

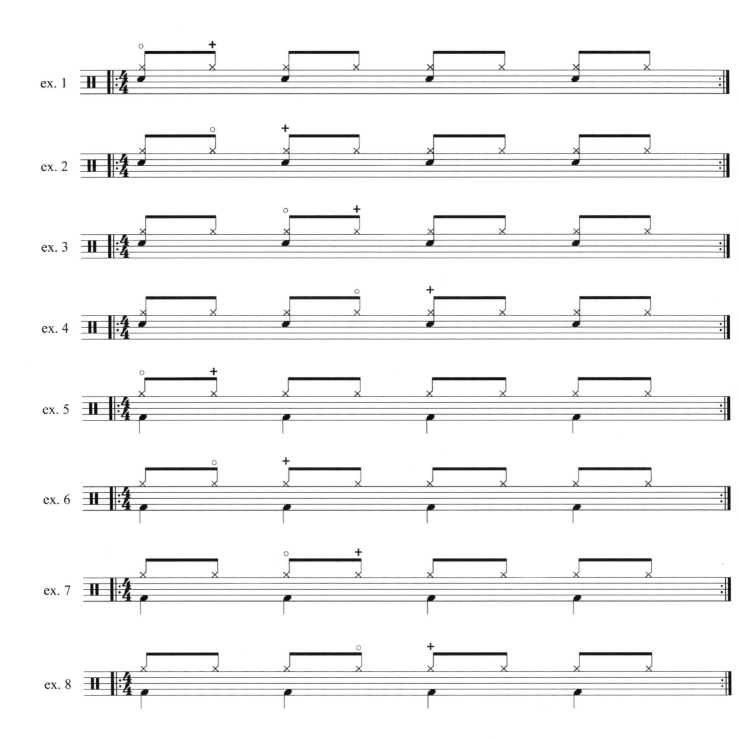

Three Voice Coordination with Open Hi-Hats

Now you can play open hi-hats in conjunction with other voices, it's time to take your skills to the next level: playing on three voices. These exercises take the dexterity and limb control you learnt in the previous examples and combine them. They all contain snare drum, bass drum and open hi-hats and are divided into four parts (a, b, c and d). Each part has the same snare drum and bass drum pattern. What changes is the position of the open hi-hats.

Tips

*   Read through each exercise first

*   Work out where the snare drums and bass drums are, and how the open hi-hats relate to them

*   Play each exercise slowly, until you are comfortable with it

Example 8c:

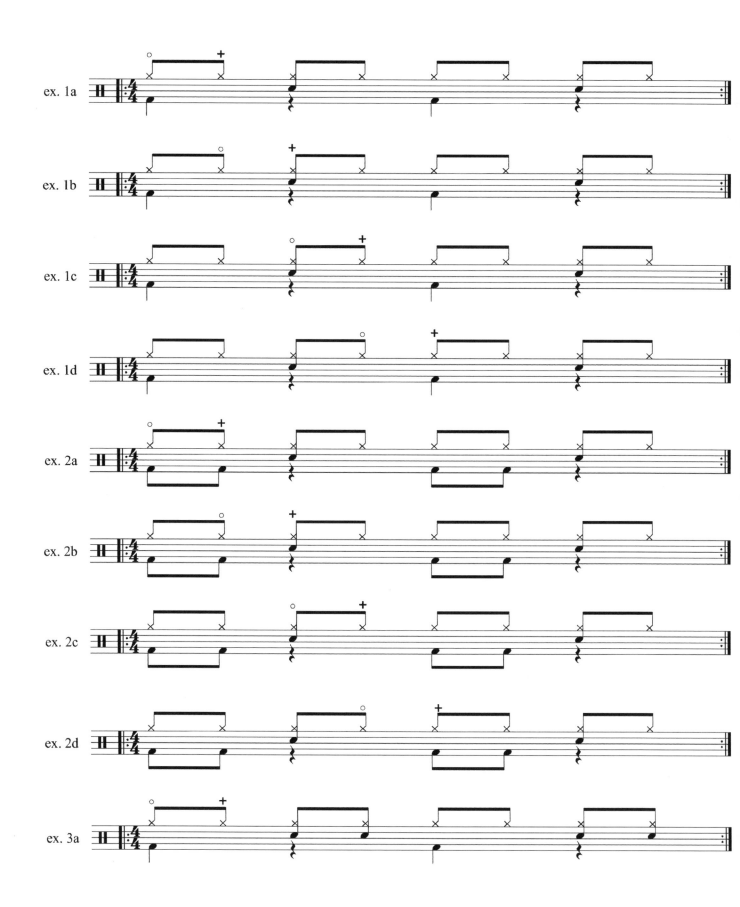

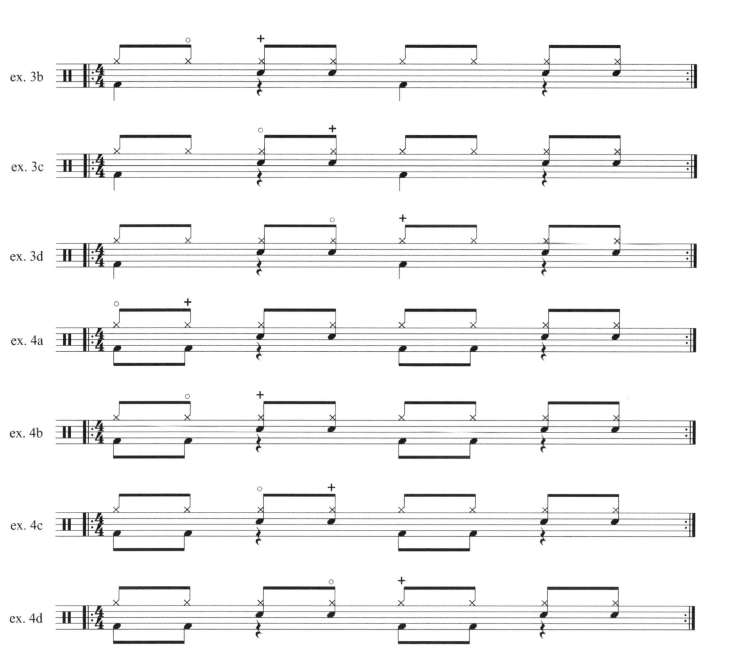

Groove Playing with Open Hi-Hats

It's time to start playing open hi-hats in some interesting grooves. Each exercise below is divided into three parts (a, b and c). Each part keeps the same groove, but changes the placement of the open hi-hats. Notice how the position of the open hi-hat affects the feel and the sound of the groove.

Tips

- Read through each exercise first and find out where the open hi-hats are before playing

- Work out the groove and how the open hi-hats relate to it

Example 8d:

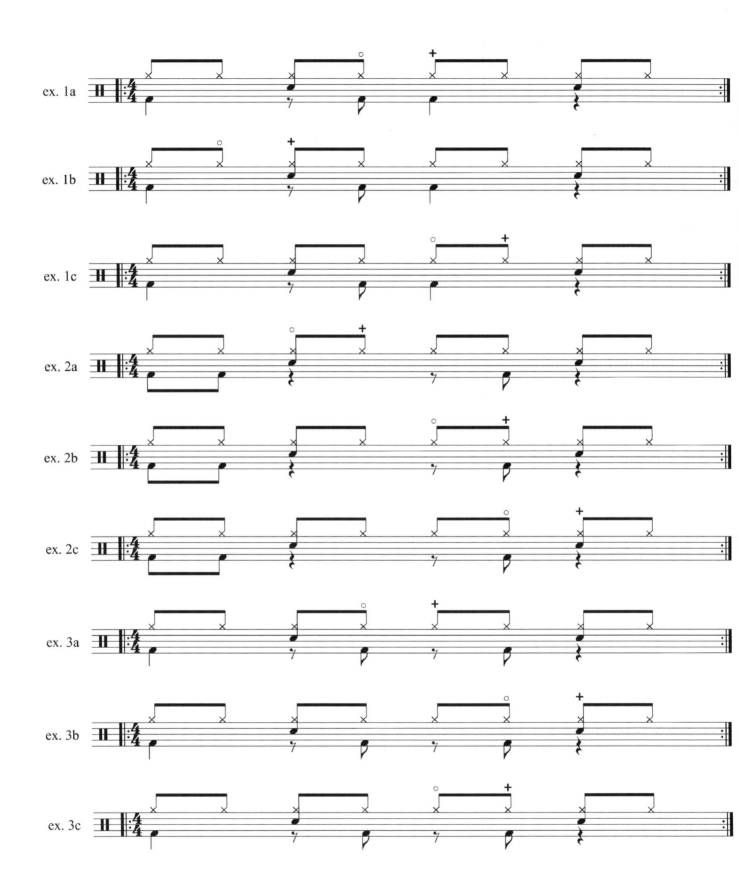

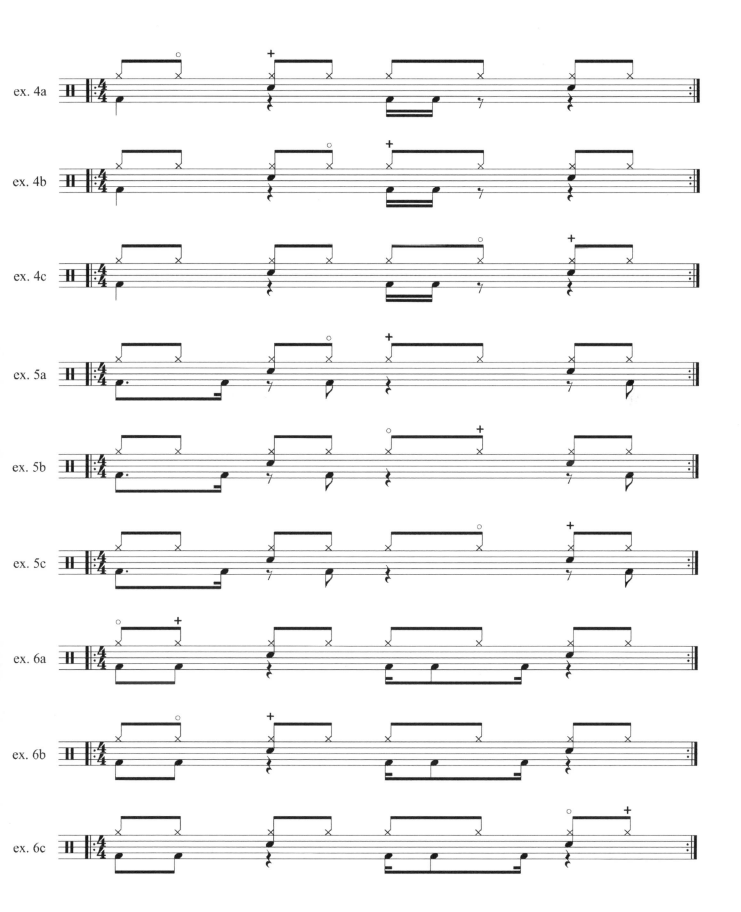

ex. 4a

ex. 4b

ex. 4c

ex. 5a

ex. 5b

ex. 5c

ex. 6a

ex. 6b

ex. 6c

You can use open hi-hats in any groove you want and position them anywhere in the bar. How you use them is up to you.

Lesson Nine – Accented Hi-Hat Patterns

Lesson Overview

This lesson focuses on the exciting possibilities of accented hi-hat patterns.

We will begin by introducing the concept of accented hi-hat patterns, how they are notated and what techniques are required. Next, we will study exercises that help you develop the movements, coordination and dexterity needed to play them. Finally, we will learn these patterns in a groove context and get you playing some fantastic music.

Accented hi-hats are an integral drumming concept with numerous possibilities. You'll learn a lot in this lesson, so let's jump right in.

Introduction to Accented Hi-Hat Patterns

Accented hi-hat patterns are a tool of great value to a drummer and add another dimension to your groove playing to create more intricate rhythmic ideas. They have been around since the invention of the hi-hat and are used in almost every musical genre.

So far, we have studied hi-hat patterns that have been played at a constant dynamic. However, hi-hat patterns do not always have to be played like this. Much like the accented snare drum rhythms, hi-hats can also be played with accents. This technique does require a high level of coordination and practising them can be frustrating. Don't let this discourage you, as accented hi-hat patterns are a versatile drumming technique.

What are Accented Hi-Hat Patterns?

Typically, accented hi-hat patterns consist of a repeated accented phrase that is played in conjunction with a groove. They add an extra rhythmic level to the groove to create more rhythmic layers and make the groove more intricate. You can think of them as a sub-groove that's articulated by harder strikes on an existing pattern.

Notation

Accents of the hi-hat are notated with a < written above the note.

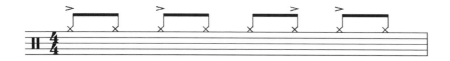

What stick position to use?

When playing non-accented hi-hats, the tip of the stick plays on the surface of the hi-hat.

When playing accented hi-hats the shoulder of the stick plays on the edge of the hi-hat.

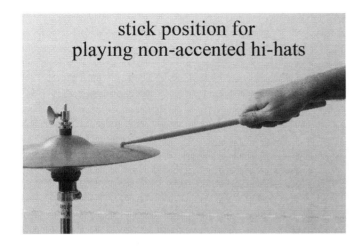

stick position for
playing non-accented hi-hats

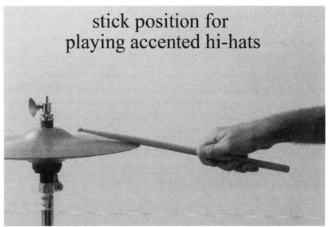

stick position for
playing accented hi-hats

There's no specific stick position for open hi-hats, so it's up to you to decide how to play them. Each stick position will affect the sound that will be produced.

What Grip Technique to Use?

Accents can be played with either the German, French or American grip, but remember that the German grip is naturally louder and makes it easier to play accents. In contrast, the French grip offers more control, making it easier to play non-accented notes.

What Strokes to Use?

Playing accents on the hi-hats requires the same strokes needed to play accents on any other part of the kit.

Playing Accented Hi-Hats

Let's learn to play some isolated accented hi-hat patterns.

Tips

- Read through each exercise first

- Work out what the accented hi-hat patterns are before playing

- Figure out which strokes to use before playing

- Concentrate on your stick positions. Make sure you are using the ones you want

Example 9a:

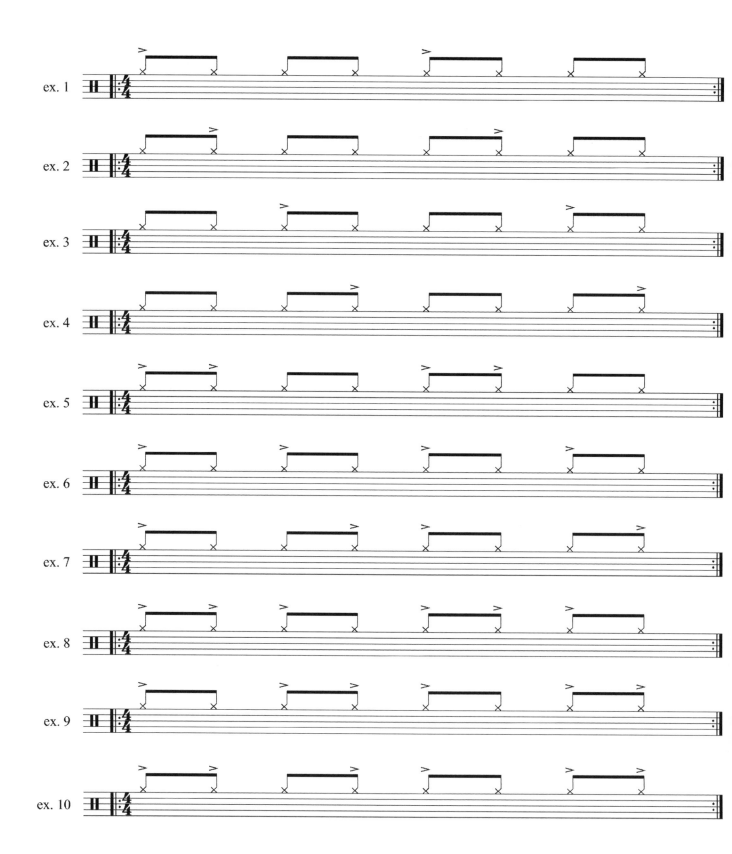

Accented Hi-Hat Patterns in Conjunction with another Voice

Now you can play isolated accented hi-hats patterns, it's time to take the next step and use them in coordination with your other limbs. Playing accented hi-hat patterns in conjunction with other voices requires a new level of dexterity and limb control and the exercises will help develop your coordination. Each exercise is played on two voices: the first four are on the hi-hat and snare drum, and the second four are on the hi-hat and bass drum.

Tips

- Read through each exercise before playing it

- Work out how the accented hi-hats relate to the other instruments being played

- Play each exercise slowly and work with a metronome to build speed and confidence

- Do not let the accented hi-hat pattern affect the snare or bass drum

Example 9b:

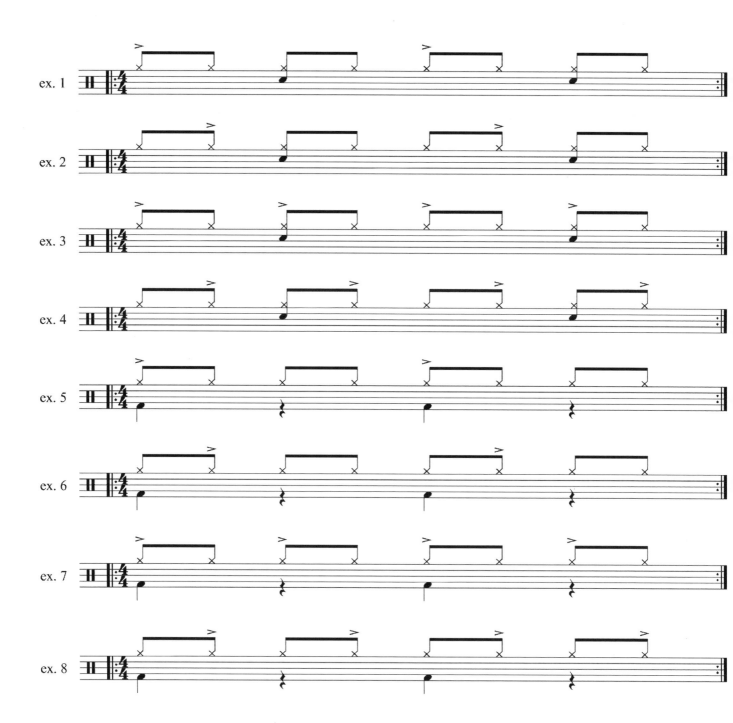

Three Voice Coordination with Accented Hi-Hat Patterns

Let's move forward and play accented hi-hat patterns with three-voices. The exercises below all contain snare drum, bass drum and hi-hats with open hi-hats and are divided into four parts (a, b, c and d). Each part has the same snare drum and bass drum pattern, but the position of the accented hi-hat pattern changes each time.

Work with a metronome to build confidence, speed and stamina.

Tips

- Read through each exercise first

- Work out where the snare drums and bass drums are, and how the accented hi-hats relate to them

Example 9c:

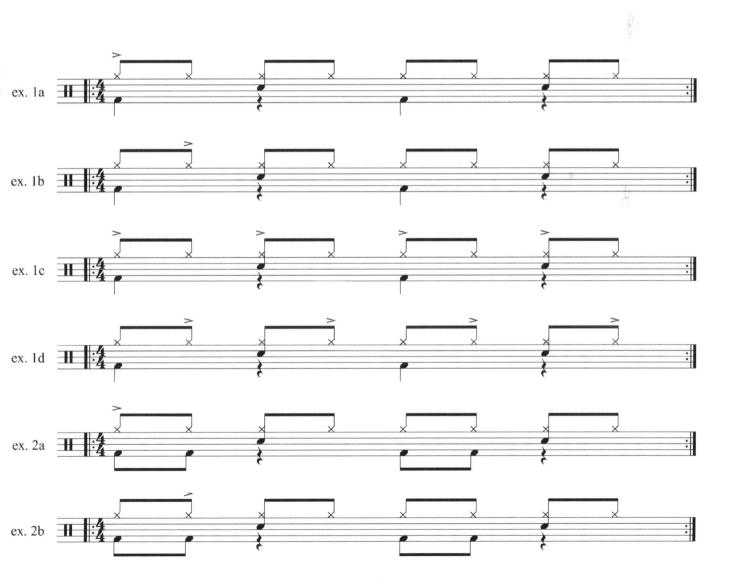

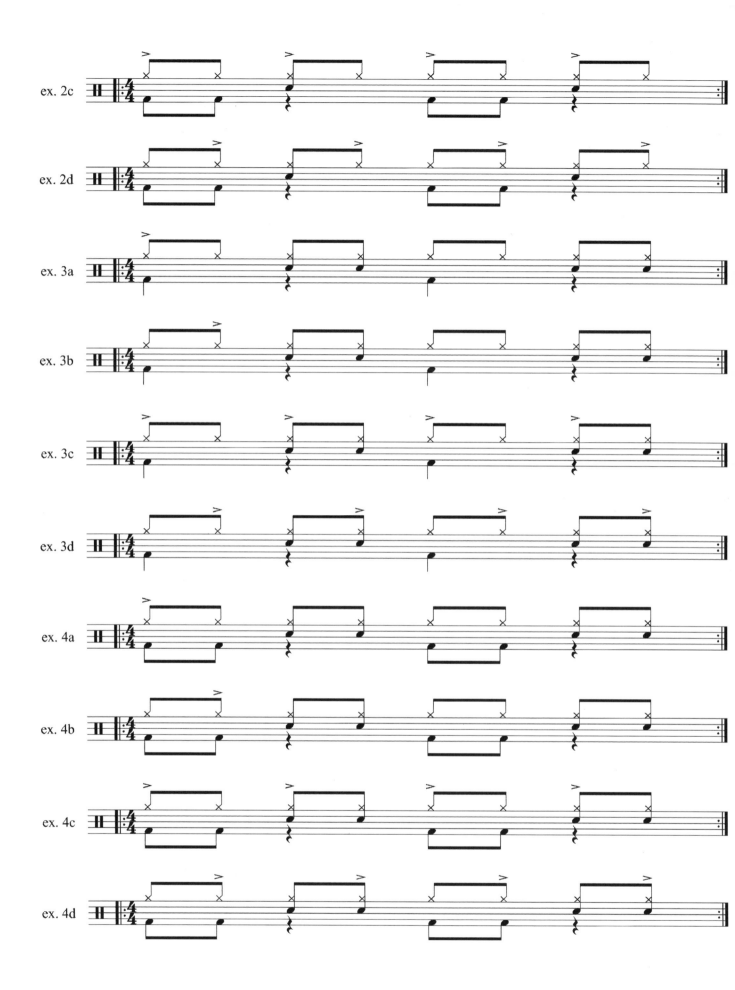

Groove Playing with Accented Hi-Hats

Now it is now time to start playing accented hi-hat patterns in a groove context. Each exercise below is divided into four parts (a, b, c and d). Once again, the accented hi-hat pattern changes on each part. Notice how the different accented hi-hat affects the feel and the sound of the groove.

You can use accented hi-hat patterns in any groove you want, and position the accents anywhere in the groove. Now that you understand the concept of accented hi-hat playing, it is up to you to decide how you want to use them.

Play through each exercise until you are comfortable with it.

Tips

- Read through each exercise first

- Work out the accented hi-hat pattern before playing

- Work out the groove, and how the accented hi-hat pattern relates to it

Example 9d:

Example 9e:

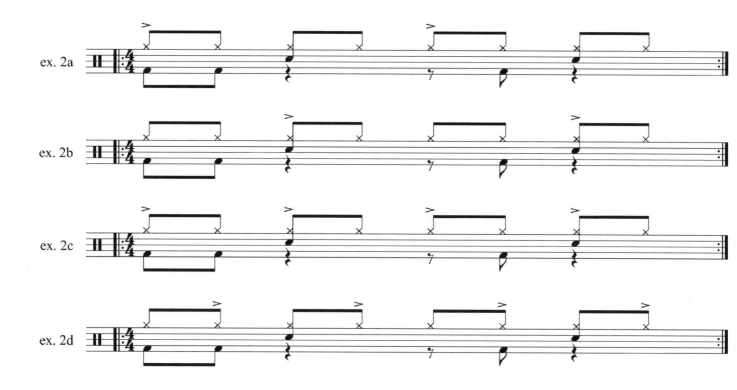

Example 9f:

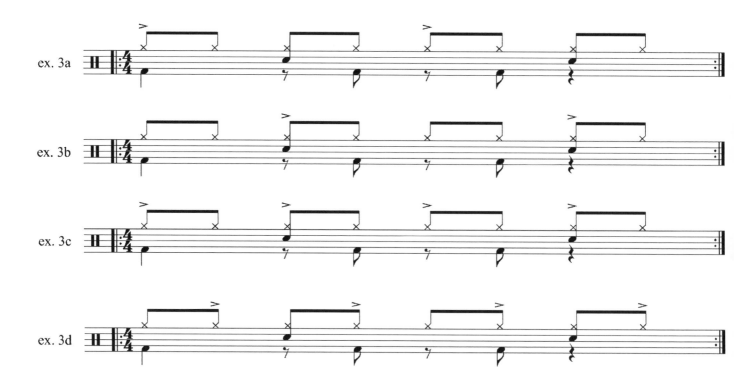

Example 9g:

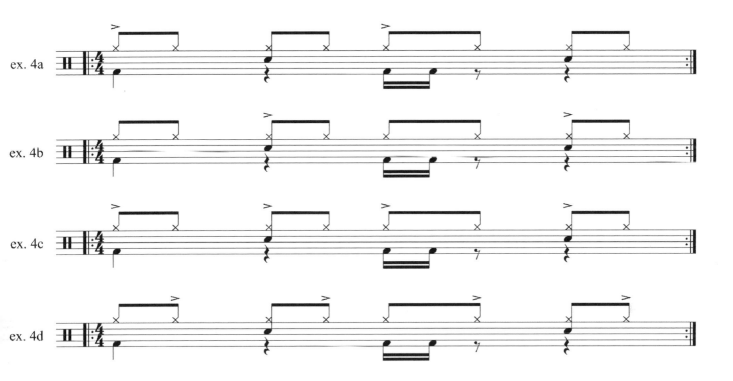

ex. 4a

ex. 4b

ex. 4c

ex. 4d

Example 9h:

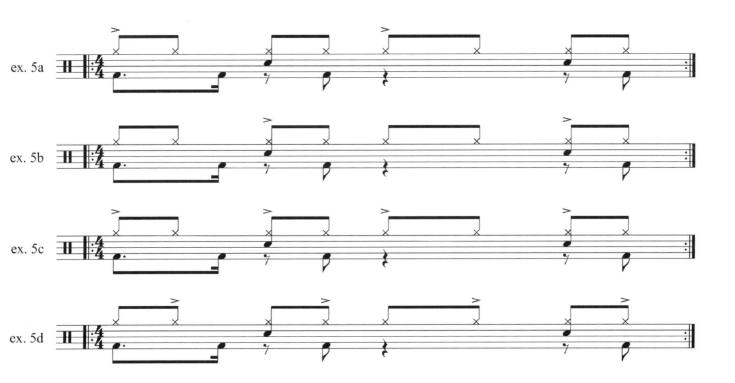

ex. 5a

ex. 5b

ex. 5c

ex. 5d

Example 9i:

Lesson Ten – Ride Lines

Lesson Overview

This lesson will look at the concept of ride lines and the techniques and skills needed to play them.

After introducing what ride lines are, we'll look at why they are used, and what the five main lines are. We'll study some exercises that get you used to their movements and build coordination and dexterity.

As always, we will start with solo voice playing before expanding to multiple voices and moving on to playing ride lines in a groove context.

Ride lines are an amazing skill to master, but, as with anything, they can be difficult to play at first because they require a high level of dexterity and coordination. However, you'll soon find that ride lines give you more rhythmic expression and artistic possibilities.

Let's begin!

Ride Line Introduction

The birth of ride lines came as soon as the ride cymbal was added to the kit. They were adopted by jazz players and became an integral part of the genre. Since then, they have permeated most genres and have become an important part of playing drums

Playing ride lines requires a high level of coordination. However, the exercises in this lesson will guide you through this concept and leave you with a good understanding of how to play them. They can be maddening to practise, but being able to play ride lines will give you more rhythmic possibilities and greater creative expression.

What are Ride Lines?

A ride line is simply the act of playing a repeated rhythmic pattern on the ride or hi-hat during a groove.

1/16th Note Ride Lines

A ride line is any repeated pattern played on the ride or hi-hat. It can be made up of any combination or denomination of note. However, the most common type of ride line is a one-beat repeated phrase based on 1/16th notes.

Below are the five most common 1/16th note ride lines. Learn each one carefully.

Tips

- Read through each exercise first

- Try each exercise on both the ride and the hi-hat

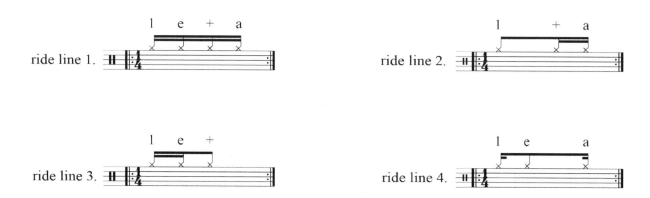

Ride Lines in Conjunction with another Voice

The forty exercises below are divided into five groups. Each group has a different ride line and consists of eight exercises to get you playing the snare drum and bass drum in conjunction with the ride lines. As always, use a metronome to help you develop confidence, rhythm and speed.

Tips

- Read through each exercise before playing it

- Work out how ride lines relate to the other voices

- Play each exercise slowly, until you are comfortable with it

- Do not let the snare drum or bass drum affect the ride line

Ride line 1

Example 10a:

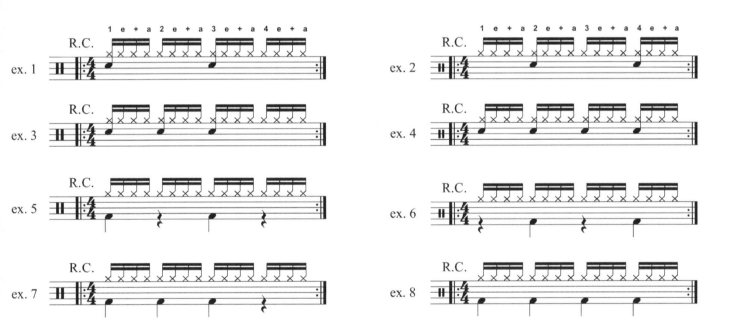

Ride line 2

Example 10b:

Ride line 3

Example 10c:

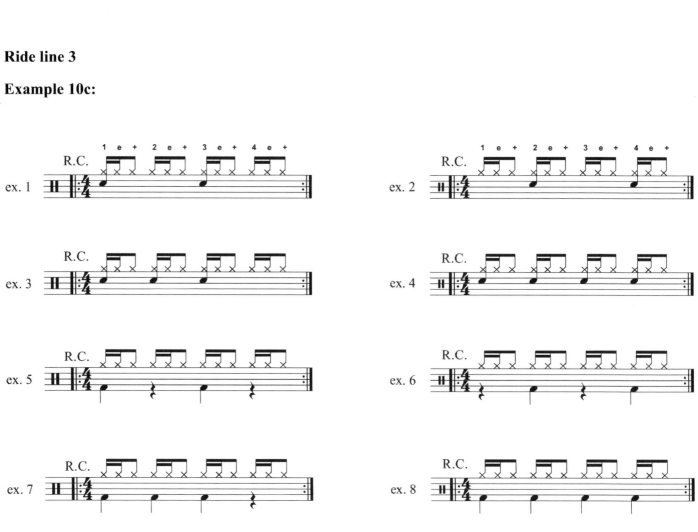

Ride line 4

Example 10d:

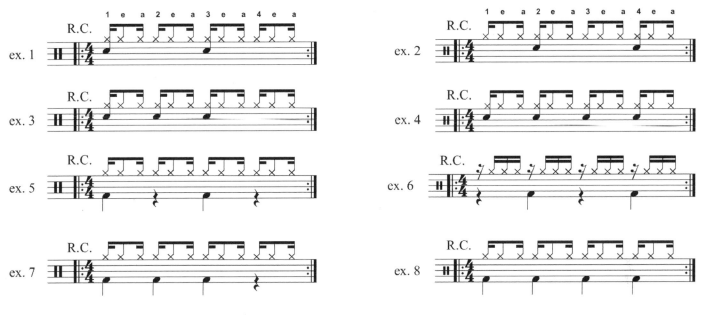

Ride line 5

Example 10e:

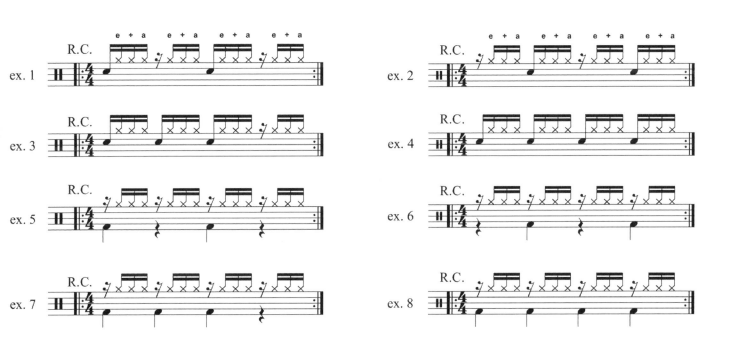

Ride Lines in Conjunction with the Hi-Hat Foot

Now that you can play ride lines in conjunction with the snare and bass drum, it's time to improve your dexterity by adding in the hi-hat played with foot. Each exercise below has a different ride line with 1/4 notes played on the hi-hat foot.

Tips

- Read through each exercise first

- Work out how the hi-hat relates to the ride line being played

- Play each exercise slowly, until you are comfortable with it

Example 10f:

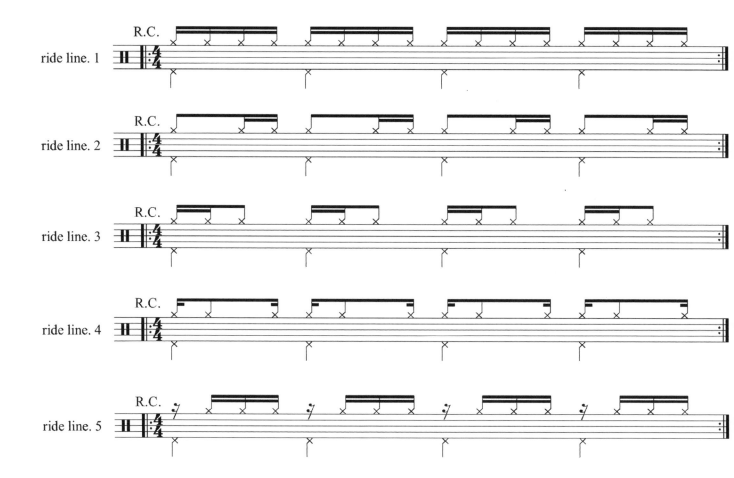

Ride Lines with Four-Way Coordination

It is now time to combine all the previous rise line coordination exercises and begin playing ride lines with four-way coordination.

The following twenty exercises are divided into five groups. Each group has a different ride line and consists of four exercises to develop your coordination. Don't forget the metronome!

Tips

- Read through each exercise before playing it

- Work out how the snare drum, bass drum and hi-hat relates to the ride line being played

- If you are struggling to play an exercise, break it down into its individual parts. Then combine the parts, one by one, until you reconstruct the complete exercise.

Ride line 1

Example 10g:

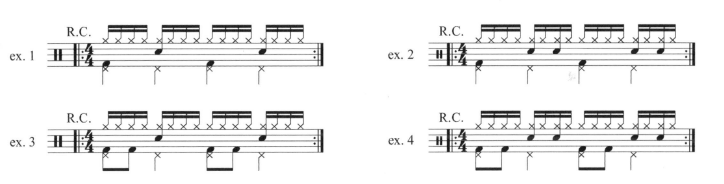

Ride line 2

Example 10h:

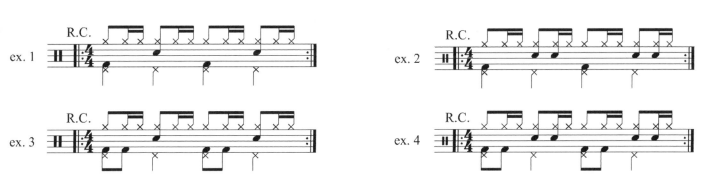

Ride line 3

Example 10i:

ex. 1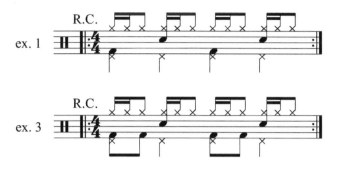

ex. 2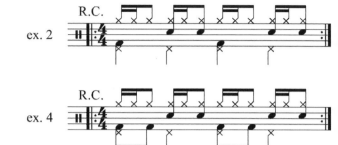

ex. 3

ex. 4

Ride line 4

Example 10j:

ex. 1

ex. 2

ex. 3

ex. 4

Ride line 5

Example 10k:

ex. 1

ex. 2

ex. 3

ex. 4

Ride Line Grooves

The final step is to use ride lines in some useful grooves.

The following forty exercises are divided into five groups. Each group has a different ride line and consists of eight grooves. The grooves in each group are identical – the only thing that changes is the ride line. Listen to how the different ride lines affect the groove.

Tips

- Read through each exercise first

- Work out how the snare drum, bass drum and hi-hat relates to the ride line being played

- Play the grooves slowly until you are comfortable

Ride line 1

Example 10l:

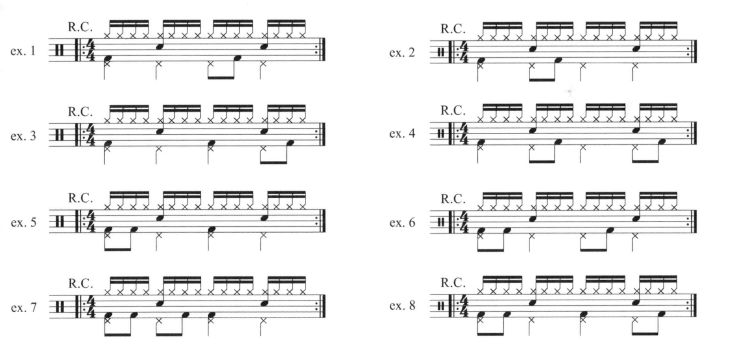

Ride line 2

Example 10m:

Ride line 3

Example 10n:

Ride line 4

Example 10o:

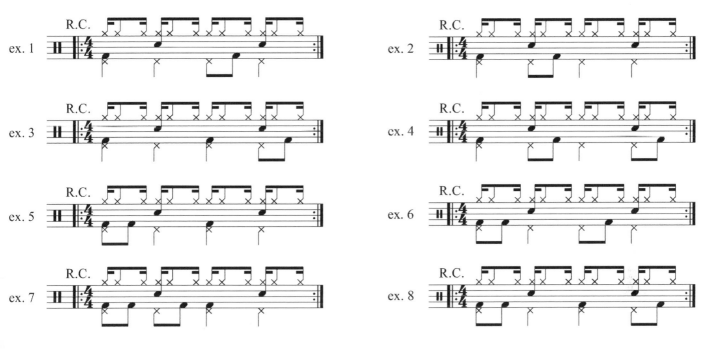

Ride line 5

Example 10p:

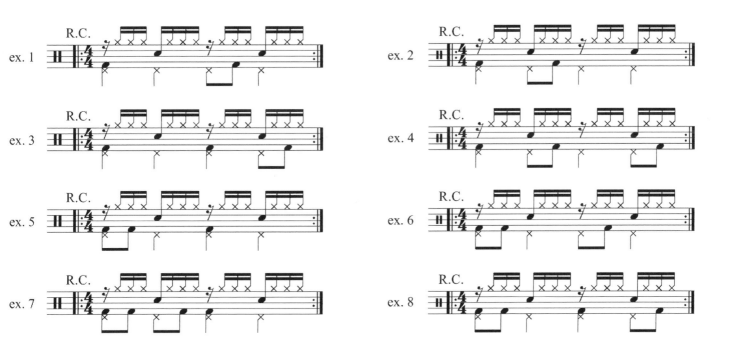

Continue your exploration of this idea by creating your own ride line grooves. You can do this by choosing any ride line you want, put a backbeat on it, and then play any bass drum pattern you desire. Don't let the end of this book be the end of your creative practice.

Keep practising, and you'll become the drummer you want to be!

About the Author

Daryl Ingleton began his musical life at a young age, starting with the trumpet at age 8. He studied this instrument for many years, until he wanted to expand his musical knowledge. He then switched instruments for many years until he found drums and percussion at the age of 15. Since then he has studied with published authors, international touring musicians and industry greats. In 2006 he was accepted into the London College of Music where he studied with some of the UK's best session players and tutors. He later graduated with a Bachelor of Music with Honours degree.

From then on he became involved with shows, bands and projects throughout London, in various different styles and situations. During this time, he also continued his independent training, always striving to learn more, which led him to travel to different continents to further his studies and pursue different avenues of the music industry.

Throughout his music life Daryl has always been eager to share his musical knowledge. Because of this he has developed an understanding of how to communicate this knowledge in a way that is easily understandable. Daryl wants every drummer to have the best understanding of their instrument possible, and these books are his effort to share the techniques and knowledge he has honed over a decade of learning and practising.

Please enjoy and take all the knowledge you can from this book series.

Thank You!

This book series has been a passion project of mine for many years. From the initial concept to the first draft, and then to the completed article, it has taken a lot of concentration and dedication.

Throughout my musical life, and through the creation of this series, I have received a lot of support from many people. I would like the thank my family (Peter Ingleton, Diana Ingleton, John Sellars, Joyce Sellars, Katrina Harling and Lauretta Hunt) who encouraged my musical education by helping find tutors and schools, and for allowing me to play for hours on end without complaint. Thanks to my first drum tutor (Dave Zubraski), who got me hooked on drums and percussion.

To all of my tutors who showed me new ideas and concepts (Erik Stams, Darryn Farrugia, drumTech and the London College of Music). To all my musical friends and peers (the Babilondon Crew, the Radstock Crew, the Just Like Little People Crew), who shared and grew their music with me. To everyone who helped with the creation of this series (Luke Hollingworth and Fundamental Changes Ltd). And to my partner (Lucie Fournaison) who always encouraged my playing and writing.

Finally, I would like to thank you, the reader, for purchasing this book and series. The information here is meant for you, and I am personally very happy that you have taken the step to further your musical education.

Other Drum Books from Fundamental Changes

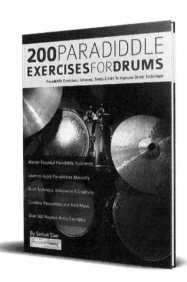

Printed in Great Britain
by Amazon

58339881R00070